Cross-Country

with **Blyth Tait**

Cross-Country

with **Blyth Tait**

KENILWORTH PRESS

First published in 2004 by
Kenilworth Press Ltd
Addington
Buckingham MK18 2JR

British Library Cataloguing in Publication Data
A catalogue record for this book is available from the British Library

ISBN 0-872119-73-5

Design and layout by Paul Saunders
Printed in Singapore by Stamford Press

PHOTO CREDITS
All photos are by David Fraser
except the following:
Stephen Sparkes, pages 98-99 and pages 108-109
Fieldhouse Riding Equipment, page 23 (left)

Contents

Acknowledgements 7

Part 1 Principles of Cross-Country Riding
The Rider's Balance 10
The Horse's Balance 13
Control 14
Power and Impulsion 14
Rhythm 15
Boldness and Confidence 15
Speed 17
Cross-Country Training 17

Part 2 Participating in Cross-Country
Equipment Used by the Horse 20
Equipment Used by the Rider 23
Horse Fitness 25
Rider Fitness 25
Walking the Course 25
Ten-Minute Box Procedure 28
After-Care for Horses 29
Horse Injuries 29

Part 3 Analysis of Cross-Country Fence Technique
Uprights 32
Spread Fences 35
Simple Log 36
Hanging Log 38
Ditches 40
    Ditch and Palisade 40
    Trakehner 42
Steps Up 44
Steps Down 46
Corner 48
Fence on an Upward Slope 50

Fence on a Downward Slope 52
Coffin 54
Bullfinch/Hedge 58
Bank Up Followed by Fence 61
    Bank, One Stride to Palisade 61
    Bank to Narrow Brush 62
Upright Followed by Bank Down 64
Water Fences 68
Bounces 77
    Bounces into Water 81
Hayrack 83
Drop Fences 84
Arrowhead 89
Combinations 90
    Upright to Spread 91
    Upright to Bounce 93
    Ditch and Palisade Drop to Palisade 94
    Related Fences 96
Sunken Road 99
Fence with Roof 100
Turning Fences 102
    Serpentine 102
    Hair-Pin Turn 104
Diagonal Line 106
Open Ditch or Water 108
Start Box 110

Part 4 Problems
Refusal 112
Run-out 114
Fall 116

Glossary 118
Index 119

Acknowledgements

One thing is certain with regard to cross-country riding – you never stop learning. Every time I train or compete I encounter new experiences that teach me more, and better prepare me for the future.

I want to say a big thank you to all the people whose photographs appear in this book, and I'd like to apologise to any of you shown in a less than flattering light. I know that, like me, you will have learned from your experiences, and I hope that, through the suggestions I put forward in the analysis of your pictures, others might learn a little too.

My thanks are due to photographer David Fraser for the great shots he took for the book, gathered at many events throughout the UK. His expertise and professionalism are much appreciated. Additional photos were kindly provided by Stephen Sparkes and Fieldhouse Riding Equipment.

Once again I am extremely grateful to all at Kenilworth Press who have been responsible for putting this book together, especially Lesley Gowers for her flair in deciphering and rearranging my jumbled words, and Paul Saunders for his excellent design and layout.

Part 1

Principles of Cross-Country Riding

Good cross-country technique requires that horse and rider possess a solid foundation in basic skills so that they can safely negotiate fixed obstacles on varied terrain and in all kinds of conditions. In Part 3 of this book I discuss specific techniques required for different types of obstacle, and on every occasion it is assumed that the basic skills are already established. Confidence, control, rhythm, balance, engagement, impulsion and rider security are all essential. These qualities complement one another and, when combined, will promote consistent results. Any deficiencies will reduce the chance of success and weaken the overall performance.

The Rider's Balance (Security and Position)

Success across country is measured by achievement. If you get to the finish you have done well. There is no definitive right way, or indeed wrong way, to ride across country but consistent success is usually born from a good fundamental base in the rider's balance and security.

Your individual riding position and technique is often the result of your physical build, coupled with the early experiences encountered when learning your craft. To some extent it is possible to manufacture a rider's position with education, but ultimately an instinctive, natural feel and genuine 'stickability' cannot be taught. It must be developed through experience and mileage. Improvement is very often as a result of mistakes - learning the hard way!

That said, the most vital aspect of any rider's position is his independence of balance. The rider's ability to remain in the saddle cross-country must not be dependent on the reins and therefore the horse's mouth. He cannot rely on the seat of his pants either, as riding in a heavy manner will tire the horse and impede his progress when negotiating the likes of

Here the rider displays a nice, secure position over a straightforward spread fence. He is in close contact with the saddle and his weight is well distributed over the centre of the horse's balance. His lower leg is underneath his upper body to give a good base of support, and his heel is well down for strength. He shows an independence of balance and is not reliant on the horse's mouth for his own security. His eyes are well up but he has dropped his hands too low for my liking. This has brought his shoulders down as well – not ideal if something unexpected occurs on landing.

banks up or drops down. Instead, the focus should be firmly on the rider's lower leg for strength and security.

When riding, just as when walking or standing, if the lower leg is beneath your bodyweight, you have a good base of support on which to balance. If the lower leg slides too far back or too far forward you will be insecure and topple easily.

The stirrups should not be too long; you need to ride with a good bend in the knee. This will enable you to absorb the impact of landing on any gradient, without banging around on the horse's back. Many people fall into the trap of believing that a longer stirrup will give them added security. The opposite is often true, as they become loose and thrown about by the horse's movements.

Your weight should be well down into your heels to make the lower leg strong, both for gripping and for giving commands to the horse. However, the knees should not grip excessively or they will weaken the lower leg and reduce its effectiveness.

Cross-country fences do not fall down when a mistake occurs, so although you should be positive and attacking at all times, you should also think defensively with your body position. Try not to push your shoulders forward on take-off as this will put your weight ahead of the horse's centre of balance, and especially so if the momentum is slightly checked. If your shoulders are pushing forward they can also cause you to pivot on your knee and lose the lower leg backwards. Instead you should be ready for any slight mistake and keep your shoulders up more than when show jumping.

If you are ever guilty of not being in the ideal centre of balance when jumping a cross-country fence then you are better to be behind the movement than in front of it, as shown here. Perhaps the approach was quicker than hoped, and as a result the rider has adopted a defensive position. He has moved his lower leg forward as a brace, and pushed his weight back, keeping his shoulders well up. This rider will not get caught ahead of the movement on landing and will be able to encourage his horse forward for the ditch that follows. He is not, however, restricting his horse as he has slipped his reins to allow plenty of freedom.

Both horse and rider have been caught out of balance in this photo, possibly as a result of hitting the top of the fence. All of the rider's security has been lost from her lower leg and she has been pitched forward. She will take the impact of landing on her knee, and as a consequence I would not wish to see the outcome of the next stride. Obviously aware of the mistakes, the rider is trying to move her shoulders back and is clinging on bravely. She has let the reins slip through her hands, giving her horse freedom to recover from his mistake. By keeping her eyes up she is giving herself the best fighting chance of remaining on board.

Because the bascule of the horse will be a little flatter across country, with the added speed and more open stride, your lower leg should stay well forward to act as a brace. If a rider were to sit anywhere other than over the centre of the horse's balance, then it would be preferable to be behind the movement than in front of it.

Just as in dressage, elasticity in the arms is very important. Straight, rigid arms will create tension and resistance in the horse. The elbows should be bent at all times, and there should be a soft, continuous line maintained from the elbow through to the horse's mouth to ensure a secure and consistent contact and good control.

Whenever you ride you should always look up and ahead. Looking down does not help with balance. Where you look is normally where you end up.

RIGHT ABOVE **At the point of take-off the rider has dramatically risen up for the jump itself. She has therefore ended up well above her horse with her weight on her toes. She has pushed her shoulders too far forward so is slightly ahead of the horse's movement. As a result the elbows have come out, and so the elastic contact through to the horse's mouth has been lost. The position is too precarious for jumping fixed timber.**

RIGHT **On landing I am momentarily caught out of balance with my horse. I have not allowed for the falling ground behind the wall fence, and as my horse has slowed considerably on landing I have been caught ahead of the movement. My shoulders have gone too far forward, and as a result my lower leg has slipped back, causing me to take the impact of landing on my knee. I am in no position to assist my horse and I am having to brace my hands on the horse's neck to stay in the saddle. I would have been better to have sat up with my shoulders, slipped the reins a little and kept my leg forward and on.**

The Horse's Balance

The balance of the horse is extremely important in cross-country riding. A well-balanced horse will have a far greater chance of successfully negotiating all the different obstacles he will encounter, and a good balance will give him confidence.

A horse jumps off his hindquarters more easily than he does off his forehand so this is something that the rider must work to develop. The rider should feel as though his horse is travelling 'uphill' at all times, as he gallops and as he makes his approach towards the fences. This 'feel' will be the result of the horse having his hocks well under his bodyweight, so that he is pushing from behind and is carrying his forehand in a light manner. It is not good for the horse to lean heavily on the bit and use his rider as a prop for his balance.

If the horse's hind legs are out behind his bodyweight it is not easy for him to generate the power and spring he needs to execute a powerful jump. You must therefore ensure that you engage your horse's frame and stride to assist him. If the hindquarters are ridden up into your hand the spring of the horse will begin to coil, which will give him the connection needed. If you were to abandon this support of the horse's balance in front of the fence you would lose the engagement. This is described as 'dropping' the horse on his forehand.

As a horse's length of stride and frame alter then so does his centre of balance. It moves further back towards his hocks as the stride is shortened, and it moves forward as he is opened up into a longer stride. The rider should endeavour to distribute his own weight as much as is possible over the centre of the horse's balance.

Travelling down a steep slope immediately after negotiating a jump, the rider still works on maintaining her horse's balance. She tries to support the horse with her reins (even though she has had to lengthen them over the jump) to prevent him from falling onto his forehand. She has her elbows bent, to avoid causing resistance, and shifts her weight back, to help keep the horse's centre of balance back towards his hindquarters. She still endeavours to engage the horse and create impulsion and power.

Perhaps this rider is making a recovery from a mistake at the first element of this combination as she is urging the horse forward here with determination and force. Unfortunately all engagement has been lost, the stride is flat and the horse's balance has been abandoned. If the pair fails to make the distance to the second element they will almost certainly suffer a mishap through their loss of balance.

Control

The rider must always have control of his horse when going across country. He must be able to regulate the speed, and to stop, start and turn easily, and be able to influence the stride pattern and energy level. When the horse removes the control from the rider's hands, run-outs, refusals and falls will occur.

At the lower levels it is all too easy to choose a more severe bit instead of training to improve the control of the horse. As the degree of difficulty of the obstacles increases as the horse rises through the grades, so too does the speed at which he must negotiate them. Without control it will be a recipe for disaster and the rider will need to continue to increase the severity of the bit.

Control is very much an issue of working with the horse and not against him – if it were to become a battle of strength then the horse, being substantially larger, would win. The rider must influence the horse's mind to respond through education and schooling as well as working to enhance the horse's balance and engagement. A stiff, wooden horse is likely to be less controllable than a supple, light one that gallops in a round, elastic manner. A horse on his forehand, or one that is heavy in the hand, will be less responsive. Similarly a horse with his head in the air and hollow in his back will probably resist the rider's aids. Good training will develop control.

Here the horse has taken control from his rider and has run out from the obstacle. Despite the short martingale and cheekpieces on the bit, the horse is tipping his head, crossing his jaw and resisting the rider's attempts to steer him. He is working against the rider instead of with him.

Power and Impulsion

Power and impulsion are the preferred substitute for speed. Speed is not always the best solution when negotiating a particular type of obstacle. Often it is better to have impulsion and power instead. Obvious fences where impulsion is required are coffins, bounces, fences on turns, and banks. If taken with too much speed these fences will not jump well. Impulsion is best described as contained energy. It is the state when the rider can instantly increase the length of the stride, the pace or the power by simply releasing the stored energy, while having complete control of the horse, perhaps even to the extent that he could bring the horse to an immediate halt if needed.

Impulsion and power should be achieved by riding the horse's hindquarters up underneath him, into the rider's controlling hand. This will encourage engagement and power while maintaining the forward flow.

If the rider's reins are flopping up and down, if the horse is strung out and disconnected, or if the horse is behind the rider's leg, there will be a lack of impulsion. There may still be substantial speed but there will not be controlled power.

A horse galloping between fences with obvious power and impulsion. The picture is of a coiled spring with the horse's hocks well up under his body and plenty of push in his hindquarters. He is in a good, light balance to meet a fence, and the rider has an excellent connection of the stride between his leg and a controlling hand.

Rhythm

Just as when riding the other disciplines of eventing, the overall rhythm across country is extremely important. Without rhythm it will be difficult to maintain the balance, control and confidence.

Erratic stop/start presentations to the obstacles may cause resistance and confusion in the horse. A good even flow throughout will promote harmony and ease.

The rhythm up to, over and away from the obstacles is important but so too is the general rhythm over the entire course. The horse will remain more responsive, will breathe easier and the efficiency will be enhanced if an overall flow is established.

Boldness and Confidence

Some horses are more naturally bold than others, just like riders!

However, if horses or riders are not inherently brave, boldness can be developed with good mileage, building confidence and trust gradually.

Most horses' and riders' phobias are directly related to previous bad experiences or a lack of understanding as to how to answer the questions posed. I used to be nervous of corner fences because I didn't really understand how to negotiate them; through indecision I landed myself and my horse in the middle of one very early in my career. It took many hours of practising corners with show-jumping poles and steady repetitive negotiation of small fixed

corners for me to overcome my fears. Now I am happy to gallop down to the biggest of Badminton corners, armed both with knowledge of how to negotiate that type of fence plus confidence from progressive development of my experience along the way.

Bravery can be both encouraged and destroyed. If, for example, a horse has never seen a ditch before it would be very unwise to ask him to attempt a deep, wide one straight off. This may test him too far and develop in him suspicion and concern. Instead it would be more sensible to be progressive and try a small one first. Once that is being negotiated well then a larger one can be attempted. The success and the knowledge gained at the small ditch will develop the braveness needed to carry the horse over the

A picture of complete harmony between horse and rider (in fact the rider's expression shows more concern than does her horse!). The horse has responded without question to his rider's requests with a fluent and bold leap. Although he has no prior knowledge of the depth of the water, he has trust in his rider.

Not every horse is naturally or immediately brave, but through careful and positive education, boldness and confidence can be developed. The surprise of two steps down from light to dark has caused this horse to become nervous and concerned. The rider keeps his eyes in the direction that he wishes to go and tries to prevent the horse from running away from the issue. With reassurance from the rider, the horse will learn to first look, assess, and then attempt the obstacle, after which he can be rewarded.

larger version. Success breeds success. Failure will only knock confidence, and bad experiences can be difficult to overcome.

If a horse is timid despite the rider's efforts to give him a good, sympathetic education, the whip can be introduced for reassurance. It should always be used immediately behind the rider's leg as an extension to the leg commands and should not be applied anywhere else.

Commitment is important. I have seen many incidents where riders have been determined and one hundred per cent committed and even though they have been doing the wrong thing they have had success. Being half-hearted will not help.

Speed

Speed is the last ingredient to be included in the recipe for success, but it should not be added before the vital elements of balance, rhythm, control and impulsion are established. If speed is introduced before these basics are in place it can lead to risky, uncontrolled riding. Success in negotiating an obstacle should not be dependent on speed alone. It will only get the rider so far for so long.

Typically, riders who achieve the fastest times across country often look as if they are totally unhurried. This is because they can totally manage the pace and are in fact choosing it instead of having it dictated by the horse. They would give a hurried impression if they were lacking in control and balance.

Fast times across country can also be the result of efficiency. Being able to turn quickly, guide the horse smoothly and approach the fences with rhythm and control will lead to no time being wasted and many seconds will in fact be saved.

The correct speed on approaching the jumps will nearly always be the pace that allows the jump to simply become part of the horse's canter. Too fast and the jump will become hurried and risky; too slow and the jump will require additional effort and energy from the horse.

No reward is gained when competing for going too fast. Riders should learn to assess pace and develop the skill to judge the speed required for each level at which they participate. This may take a bit of practice but if the rider is able to manage his horse then he will soon be able to influence the speed as well.

Cross-Country Training

The old saying, 'there is no substitute for experience' rings very true when it comes to cross-country riding. Working at home on developing technique is very important, but equally so is the mileage gained through practice on cross-country courses elsewhere. Cross-country schooling should be very progressive, with much care taken to ensure that new problems are introduced gradually. This will help to build the vital ingredients of trust and confidence in both horse and rider.

It is never really too early to begin cross-country schooling at a low level, but a strong foundation should be developed before tackling anything of substantial dimensions. If a rider is inexperienced then it is often a good idea to be accompanied by someone with more knowledge. The same applies to the horse. It is amazing how much confidence a green horse will gain from following an established horse tackling hazards such as water, ditches, etc.

If the horse is still unbalanced at canter and not well established in his flatwork it may even be wise to make his initial approaches to some fences in trot. He may then be better balanced and have the necessary time to assess the problems he encounters before responding. After a few attempts he will probably be cantering confidently over most fences.

Training is the time to teach horses and riders, not to test them – that is the job of competitions, much as an exam is the time to test a student's knowledge and learning. It would be unwise to send a pupil to an exam without first teaching him the answers, formulas or methods of solving potential problems. The same will apply to competing cross-country. First the homework must be done. To miss out any stages of education or take too many unnecessary risks when schooling can often cause loss of confidence and set back progress. It is harder to rebuild confidence or trust after a fright or mistake than it is to develop it in the first place.

Being progressive in training is important to overall development but can also be useful if applied to specific goals. When schooling combinations, for example, I will sometimes break up a sequence of efforts and pick out just one part to begin with. The 'out' rail of a coffin, for example, might be tackled first, then the ditch, followed lastly by the 'in' rails, ditch and 'out' rails all as one. This way I more often than not finish with a good experience and as a result walk away happy and confident. Another example would be when water schooling. First I would walk the horse into the water to show him that the bottom is firm and safe. I might then trot in and around the water before cantering in and out. If all was going well to this point, with the horse unconcerned, I might jump in off a step, then from a small jump. The end result is that I finish jumping fluently and confidently into water with a horse that trusts me. It may take a little longer but instead of testing my horse's bravery I am actually making him brave.

It is very important to have your horse's utmost trust when going cross-country. Mileage and practice can achieve this. I often explain to students when teaching, that I imagine that if I asked my horse to jump off a six-foot bank into a swollen river that was twenty feet deep then he would. It would, however, probably be the first and last time as I would totally destroy the trust in me that I had spent years developing through schooling.

In the early stages it may be necessary to school quite frequently until a good understanding has been achieved, but even once a horse is well on in his competitive career it can still be a good idea to have the odd refresher lesson. I rarely train my advanced horses over fixed fences of substantial dimensions but quite often pop them over small novice jumps such as sunken roads, coffins, trakehners, etc. to keep them attentive and confident.

Balance, control, impulsion, straightness, etc. can be worked on forever in the confines of an arena, but the true measure of achievement will be apparent when out in the country taking on fixed fences on varying gradients. When these ingredients are combined with experience, confidence, and trust through training, success will be near.

There is no substitute for experience, so mileage through practice out on cross-country courses is essential to develop trust and confidence.

Here a novice horse is happily training over steps down. The education was very progressive. First the steps were taken going upwards, then the steps were attempted downwards by themselves and finally the log at the top was included.

Initially the horse was hesitant and uncoordinated in his efforts but with repetition he was soon jumping with fluency and ease.

Cross-country schooling should be used as a chance to educate the horse, not to test him. The competitions you enter will be a measure of the training you have achieved through your work at home. In this photo the students (both horse and rider) are under the tutelage of a more experienced rider. They were accompanied throughout the session by a couple of seasoned horses, on hand to offer a lead to the youngster if extra reassurance was needed.

Part 2

Participating in Cross-Country

Equipment Used by the Horse

Saddles

Just like people, saddles come in many shapes and sizes, and so the type and make used for cross-country will be very much a personal choice. Most will choose on the basis of rider comfort and suitable fit for the horse, but in general the saddles will be forward-cut jumping ones of a lightweight nature. (See photo, page 23.)

Personally I prefer a close-contact saddle that will allow me to feel near to my horse with both my legs and seat. I do not like to feel as though I am sitting too far above the horse's back, or to feel that I am restricted in my ability to communicate with him through my legs. Thick and stiff flaps are undesirable as they will prevent this and limit the potential for grip.

It is important that knee rolls at the front of the saddle are not too bulky as it will be necessary for the rider's stirrup length to be adjusted to different heights between the various phases of the endurance test as well as the show jumping. As a result the rider's knee position will vary against the saddle flaps, so flexibility will be needed. Some riders like the security of chocks or wedges behind their leg to prevent the lower leg from slipping back, but this is something that I don't like.

Nowadays there has been a move away from a deep seat and high cantle, with a swing towards a much flatter version. This allows the rider more freedom to move his upper body position when required, in relation to the type of obstacle being negotiated. Provided that the rider has good security and balance through his lower leg he can then move his weight back for drops as well as move forward when tackling steps and banks up.

Obviously, the saddle must fit the horse well. It should not press down upon or pinch the horse's wither or it will prevent him from using his shoulders and performing well. There should be good general distribution of the rider's weight on the horse's back through the seat. A narrow or uneven contact will cause soreness. The size of the seat of the saddle should be relevant to the rider's seat.

The leather used is often grained on the surface to offer some adhesion when the saddle is wet, from either rain or splashing through water obstacles. Smooth leather can be more slippery.

I am not a fan of aluminium or lightweight stirrups but prefer heavier ones. If a stirrup is momentarily lost the lighter ones can be difficult to retrieve quickly. The heavier ones tend to hang down straighter. Rubber grips fitted into the irons can help to prevent the rider's foot from slipping out.

All stitching on the saddle should be checked regularly, particularly on the stirrup leathers. The leathers themselves should be sturdy and strong.

Girths should be soft against the horse, to avoid pinching. My preference would be the type with elastic at one end. These should not be over-tightened but will secure the saddle while offering some expansion when required by the horse during exertion. An overgirth or surcingle can be added for further security.

Bridles

The same bridle can effectively be used for all three disciplines, perhaps with a change of bit if needed. Good quality leather is a must, as the last thing you need is a snapped rein approaching a difficult fence!

Nosebands can vary from the simple cavesson through to more complicated ones, like the Grakle, dropped noseband, or to the Kineton (which works in conjunction with the bit).

Flash nosebands work on a variety of horses, and I like the top strap to be done up quite firmly, as this helps prevent the horse opening his mouth, while the bottom strap can afford to be a little less firm and so not interfere with the movement of the bit or the horse's breathing.

I prefer to use rubber reins as they are less likely to slip through the hands when wet, and give a good, consistent connection with the horse's mouth. I find web reins are just too soft and flexible and the connection is not easily kept even.

Stitching must be checked regularly and the leather kept clean and conditioned. Buckles and billets are more practical than stitching the leather, especially if you use the same bridle for different horses, as bits can quickly and easily be changed.

When going cross-country it is a good idea to undo the reins at the buckle – tie a knot in them and then do up the buckle again. If the buckle happens to come undone, you have a back-up with the knot, and it also is something a little more robust to hang onto in a tricky situation!

Martingales

Running martingales are the only type of martingale allowed cross-country.

Rubber stoppers should be used on the reins to stop the rings getting caught on the buckles. I also use a rubber stopper on the strap that comes between the horse's front legs, where the neck strap joins it, to stop it dangling too low, which could cause a leg to get caught.

Running martingales should not be fitted too tightly and, of course, will be no use if they are too long. They should be used to prevent the horse from raising his head too high, not to pull it down. Often a tight martingale can have an adverse effect as restriction will cause resistance.

Standing martingales can be useful when training but must be removed for competition.

Breastplates

For cross-country I prefer to use a racing breastplate made of elastic, with leather straps on each end, which I slide over the first two girth straps before doing up the girth. They should be attached high up on the girth so as to not restrict the movement of the horse's shoulders. Too often they are seen hanging low near the rider's feet. I would never compete without a breastplate. They are my saddle's 'safety belt' to ensure that it does not move back on the horse.

Bits

I am not a fan of complicated bits and gadgetry – a whole book could be written dedicated to bits alone. There are many different types, all with different effects. I find simple is best and most horses will go kindly in a normal snaffle, if they are well trained and well balanced.

Bitting the horse up is one way to avoid addressing the root of the initial balance or control problems. I would never dream of using anything other than a snaffle on a novice or intermediate horse, preferring to spend the time to train him at that level. Making the optimum time at that stage is not a priority, and speed can be added easily once the other ingredients in the recipe for success – such as balance, control and rhythm – are achieved. Many times the lack of control is a result of bad balance and what is going on in the horse's brain, not because he has a hard mouth.

Make sure the bit sits evenly in the horse's mouth and there is enough room either side – about a quarter inch – so that it does not pinch. It should not be too low either or it could bang on his teeth.

RIGHT **This is a selection of bits that I commonly use for cross-country.**

They range from very mild in the foreground to more severe towards the back.

The first bit in front is a straightforward loose-ring snaffle with a single joint. It has a kind, soft, metal mouthpiece.

Next is a simple eggbutt snaffle, also with a single joint.

The third bit is another snaffle but contains a French link in the centre of the mouthpiece. This has a slightly more severe nutcracker action than the single link.

Next is a three-ring gag. This will bring some pressure to the horse's poll to assist with lightness and roundness. The reins can be attached to either ring on the lower shank. The higher ring will be less severe.

A sweet-iron gag follows. I have had great success with this bit. Again it has the gag effect on the poll, and with the two joints and small rings in the middle of the mouthpiece it discourages horses from leaning on the rider's hands.

Lastly, a vulcanite pelham, which I might use on a horse that is heavy or one that pulls excessively. The chain will work to prevent the horse from crossing his jaw. It has 'cheaters' attached to the side rings to allow just one rein to be used.

Boots and Bandages

I like to use boots on the horse's legs. There are many types on the market nowadays and they can provide great protection. Most have an inbuilt pad that covers the tendons and front of the cannon bones; and they are made from durable materials that will last as well as clean easily.

The boots must fit properly to prevent rubbing or chafing. Buckles must always be on the outside of the leg and the straps need to face backwards.

Bandages, if used, must be applied correctly to prevent them slipping, and the ends must be stitched to stop them unraveling while in action, which can be dangerous. They must be applied with even pressure to avoid causing damage to the tendon, and if fitted well can offer some support to the fetlock joints.

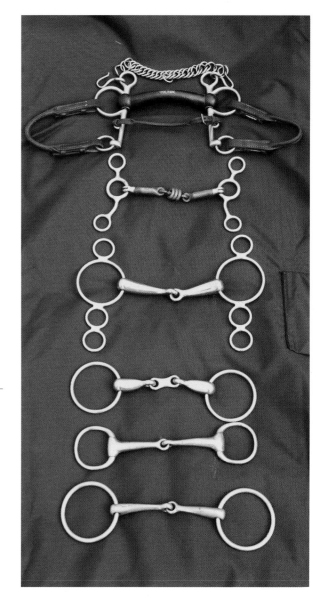

If using over-reach boots, care must be taken that they are not too long or the horse may step on one with a hind foot and trip himself up. Rubber ones can be trimmed to fit quite easily, and there are other types made out of man-made materials that work effectively too. Vaseline applied to the top rim will prevent rubs to the horse's pasterns.

A horse wearing simple kit for cross-country.

He has a leather bridle with a flash noseband and loose-ring snaffle. The reins are covered with rubber to offer grip.

He has a racing breastplate that is well fitted, with the end attachments up under the saddle flaps. They will cause no restriction to the horse's shoulders or get in the way of the rider's legs.

The saddle is lightweight, slightly forward cut and is a close contact type. The girth is soft and the surcingle has an elastic extension. The stirrups contain rubber grips.

On the horse's forelegs are soft wrap-around boots for protection, as well as rubber over-reach boots. On his hind legs are leather boots with buckles on the outside, the straps pointing towards the back. On the inside, the boots reach from the base of the hocks right down to the fetlocks.

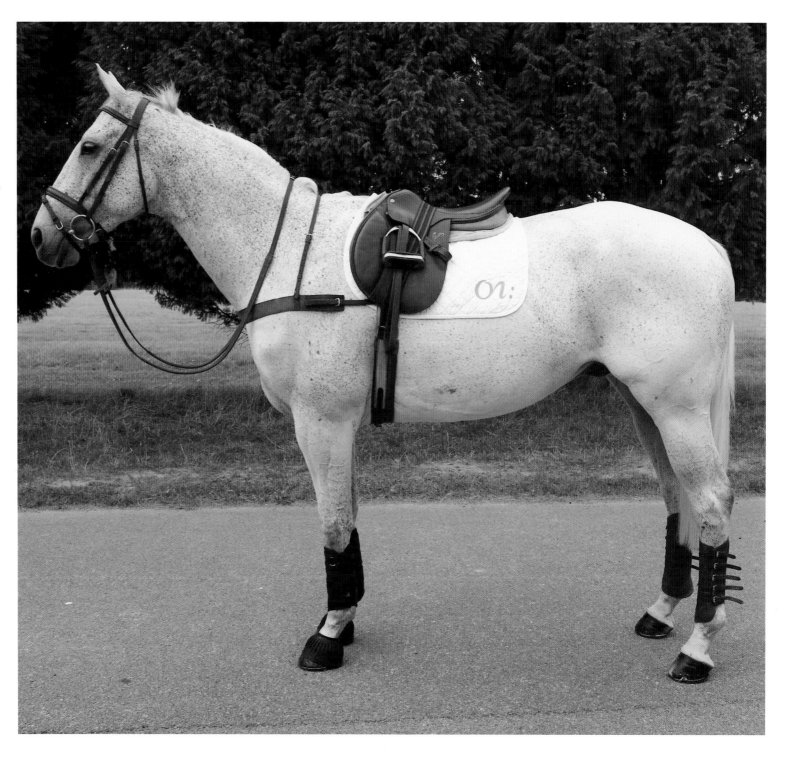

Studs

A good selection of studs should be kept in a separate box along with a small pot of grease, cotton wool, adjustable spanner and screw tap. Different studs will suit different conditions and I **always** use studs when going cross-country.

Small, spiky ones are used if the ground is hard, to break the firm surface, and large, round ones are used when it is wet or the ground is loose and shifty.

I only ever put one stud on the front feet, about halfway up on the outside. A stud on the inside increases the chance of the horse studding himself, and it is one less to be trodden on with if you fall off!

I like two studs behind, about two thirds of the way back on the shoe on each side.

Leg Grease

I normally use leg grease only at three-day events and big one-day competitions. Specially prepared event grease can be applied to the horse's legs to help him slide safely over the rough timber of cross-country fences should he connect with any jump.

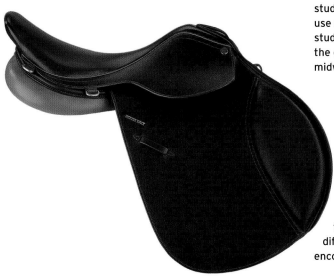

A stud is screwed into a front shoe. I do not like to use a stud on the inside of the horse's front feet and will only use a small stud on the inside of hind feet. Wearing large studs on the inside increases the risk of the horse injuring the opposite leg. The stud hole on the front shoe is midway forward on the outside.

The modern cross-country saddle will have a flat seat to allow the rider freedom to adapt his upper body position for the many and varied obstacles he will encounter. This saddle is slightly forward cut but does not have restrictive knee-rolls. This will enable the stirrup length to be adjusted to accommodate the different phases of the endurance test. The saddle will encourage close contact of the rider's seat and leg.

Equipment Used by the Rider

Helmets

Racing skull caps are a must for the cross-country as they are hard and durable and offer the best protection. They must have a chin strap and be safety standard approved. If you have a fall and knock your head it is advisable to have your helmet checked and replaced if necessary; helmets do not last forever. It is essential that a hat is always worn cross-country, whether competing or schooling, and most people will cover it with a silk to look smart.

Back Protector

As there are many back protectors on the market it comes down to personal preference but they must be safety standard approved and comfortable.

Shoulder pads are a wise option but not compulsory. The back protector should not inhibit any movement while riding – some brands are too long and restrict the rider's ability to fold at the waist. To be effective, though, they should be close-fitting and not loose.

Whips

The cross-country whip is of medium length (approximately 90cm); it needs to have a good rubber grip handle and two leather flaps on the end. It should not be too thin as it is unacceptable to cut or leave welts on the horse. The whip should nearly always be used immediately behind the rider's leg to educate the horse to respect the leg better. It should not be used aggressively by the rider out of frustration or anger. The rider should learn to carry his whip as effectively in each hand.

Spurs

Spurs come in many different designs, but the bigger and longer they are, the more likely you are to mark your horse. It is therefore preferable to use short, blunt spurs as they are only meant to be used as an extension of your leg aid and not as a weapon! A well-fitted spur should sit just under your ankle bones and be horizontal with the heel of your boot. Spurs sitting too low will be of no effect. I tend to use small spurs on all my horses cross-country as a habit.

Boots

Well-fitting and comfortable boots are essential. Made-to-measure leather boots are recommended as they will fit your individual needs. Remember that when your leg is in the jumping position you don't want your boot to catch you behind the knee. A good sole with rubber gripping on the bottom is essential so your foot doesn't slip out of the stirrup too easily. A good heel to the boot is also a must to prevent the foot from slipping through the stirrup.

Gloves

Apart from keeping your fingers warm in the cold, gloves can increase the sensitivity of feel you have on the horse's mouth. Woollen gloves with rubber-pimpled palms are highly recommended as they stop the reins from becoming slippery when the horse's neck gets sweaty. Leather gloves are more suited to dry conditions because if both gloves and reins get wet the reins will just slip through your hands.

Watch

A good-quality reliable stopwatch is a must at the upper levels for cross-country. A stopwatch is not allowed at Novice level, and I never wear one at one-day events at any level, preferring the horse to travel within its means. Riding to the clock at this stage can tempt a rider to push the horse out of his rhythm and balance. Riding too fast can cause loss of control.

I do use a stopwatch at all levels of three-day events.

The face display needs to be large, with big digits that can be easily read when you are galloping along. Make sure the stopwatch strap can secure the watch firmly on your wrist as you don't want it sliding around. The start, stop and reset buttons should require a firm press to activate them otherwise the watch could accidentally be bumped off while on your cross-country round. Having a minute beeper is helpful as it enables you to hear where you are without looking down.

Number Cloth/Medical Armband

For competition riding both the number bib and medical armband are compulsory.

Your number bib should be comfortable to wear without having straps flapping around. Medical cards should be filled in correctly so that, if needed, the medics have any relevant information on hand. Again, the medical card should be fitted comfortably and securely.

Some of the equipment used by riders on cross-country.
A well-fitted crash helmet (here with a silk cover) with a safety fastened chin strap.
A chest and back protector that does not inhibit movement. Also, non-slip gloves, whip with a rubber grip, and digital stopwatch.

Horse Fitness

As long as a few basic principles are followed, suitable fitness for cross-country should be simple to achieve. The workload should always be gradual, the horse should be sufficiently fit for the stress he is placed under and the fitness programme should not be too rigid.

A lightweight thoroughbred will probably require less fitness work than a more heavyweight warm-blood, and if the horse is competing at only a few novice one-day events he will need less work than a horse heading for a four-star three-day event. Unnecessary wear and tear on the horse's legs will reduce the length of his career, but it is probably a better fault to be too fit than not fit enough. Major injuries to tendons and ligaments are usually a result of a lack of fitness for the demands they are placed under.

There are many successful systems for getting a horse fit and most riders will adapt a programme to best utilise their available time and facilities.

A good base foundation of fitness can be achieved first through hacking and flatwork. The horse's legs and muscle tone should be conditioned before any fast work is done.

I use a combination of long, slow work, such as trotting on hills, with an interval-training programme of set canter periods. I particularly like interval training as it is based around a five-day cycle of stress and recovery. It is very progressive, and it is simple to monitor improvement and recognise problems.

I map out a programme by establishing the time I want optimum fitness and working back from there. Plenty of time should be allowed to ensure that any little set-backs, such as a stone bruise or a period of bad weather, will not matter. This is where it may be necessary to alter the programme a little, being careful not to force the fitness period quicker than the horse can cope with.

Rider Fitness

There is no point in having your horse fully fit for the cross-country, only to let the partnership down by being out of shape yourself. The best way to get fit is to ride. Fitness canters and conditioning exercise such as hill work, are especially useful, although even dressage will help tone and develop the right muscles. If it is not possible for you to do plenty of riding then you may need to supplement your fitness with running, swimming or cycling. The method you choose does not matter as long as better fitness levels are achieved. It is important not only that good cardiovascular fitness is reached but also that the rider should be well muscle toned and supple. Often a cross-country course will contain fences towards the end of the track that require control and accuracy and if the rider is out of breath and fatigued, he will be in no position to assist and direct the horse. He must still react quickly, mentally and physically, to ensure a safe and successful negotiation.

Although I ride several horses each day I still try to get to the gym three times a week to do extra work, which takes quite a bit of discipline but is worth the effort.

Walking the Course

Walking the course is the time to formulate the game plan for your ride. It is the time to learn all the routes and options, to check flag placements and to analyse the problems presented.

Taking someone with you – a friend with sound knowledge or a fellow competitor – can be beneficial. Two eyes and minds can often be better than one but you should concentrate on the job in hand and not get distracted by others. You could miss something important.

Remember that your horse will not get the opportunity to walk the course, so try to see things from his perspective as well. Your first impressions of a fence will probably be how he will react also.

Knowing your horse will enable you to choose the best lines and options for his particular strengths and weaknesses. Listen to what others might suggest regarding the obstacles, but make your own decisions and stay committed to them. Many of my most stupid mistakes have been when I have changed my mind from my initial intentions.

Look for the most economical route between the fences to save time and energy but also pay attention to the footing. The most direct line may not always be in the horse's best interests. The footing may change during the competition, so pay attention to the weather conditions and your running order. Another consideration should be the time of your ride in relation to the time you walk. Ideally you should walk on the previous day at the same time as your ride, but this will not always be practical. Work out how the sun position may alter, and the effect the shadows will have on the look of the fences.

Pay attention to the numbering of the whole course as well as at specific obstacles. Be sure to know the sequence of fences as well as the make up of each element in combinations and alternatives.

After completing your course walk try to establish an overview of the entire course. This will help to raise awareness of where the difficult sections are, where the steep or slow sections are, so that these can be incorporated into the game plan. For example, you will want to save some energy if there is a steep incline towards the end or make up lost time in the galloping sections. An alternative route or two may need to be considered to keep confidence up.

Be positive when walking the course. Don't always look at the negative consequences but look instead at what might go right!

Walking the course to establish the best line of approach and to assess all the problems that the course presents. The distances between the elements of this combination are paced out to determine the best striding options for tackling the fence.

I continually look up on the line I will eventually take to familiarise myself with the picture I will see when I ride.

Riding tactics will be based on the information learned from walking the course.

Ten-Minute Box Procedure

To enable the ten-minute box to run smoothly and efficiently you need to be **organised** and have **good time management**. Time is of the essence, but a simple approach and some forward planning will help to make things run smoothly.

Having assistance in the ten-minute box makes the job easier, but keep it to a minimum as overcrowding can be a hindrance to both horse and rider. Your helpers should know exactly what is required of them so no time is wasted when the horse arrives.

The person in charge should have a reliable watch set at the same time as the official competition clock.

A good location in the ten-minute box should be organised well beforehand. Bearing in mind that there is going to be more than one horse in the ten-minute box at a time, it is important to have your work area in a good spot, e.g. not too far away from the water supply, TV monitor and start box, in the shade if hot, etc. and not squashed in next to someone else. A waterproof rug is useful for laying all your spare gear on, and if need be to cover the gear if it rains. It also allows you to know exactly where everything is so you do not waste time if anything is needed urgently.

Ten-Minute Box Countdown

10 minutes
The horse arrives in the ten-minute box. All horses have their temperature and heart rates recorded on arrival by the officiating competition vets. While the vets are doing their job this is your first chance to loosen tack, i.e. noseband/overgirth/girth.

Without getting in the way, one of your helpers could check the horse's shoes and studs.

Removing any tack is not recommended as there are no guarantees that the horse will stand still when you want to tack up again. This is a good chance also to find out how the course is riding and if there are any specific problems. Make sure the person giving the advice is someone who is familiar with horse and rider and has a good knowledge themselves.

10–6 minutes
Sponge the horse on his neck, girth, under the saddle blanket and between the back legs. Avoid wetting the tack as much as possible. If it is a hot day there is no need to cover the horse. However, if there is a cool breeze it is a good idea to place a sweat-sheet over his loins to avoid a chill on his kidneys. Get the horse moving – do not let him stand for too long to get cold and stiffen up. He can rest after the cross-country.

6 minutes
All horses have a second vet inspection before they are cleared to start the cross-country, so if you haven't been checked go and see the vet. Do not be afraid to go to them as they aren't the ones who incur time penalties if you are late to start phase D!

4 minutes
Tighten all tack.

Apply grease to the horse's legs only! **Do not** get grease on the tack. On a warm day a minimum amount of grease should be used as too much prohibits the horse from sweating. Cover the important areas only, such as the forearms and stifles.

3 minutes
Mount the horse in plenty of time to have a quick trot/canter before making your way to the start box. It is better to get on too early than too late. I sometimes get on four or five minutes before the count down, and walk quietly before warming up.

If your horse is difficult to get into the start box, have someone on hand to help you. You are allowed to have the horse led into the start box.

0 minutes
Good luck!

Ten-minute box equipment

- Buckets
- Sponges
- Sweat scraper
- Scissors and tape
- Hole punch
- Vet kit
- Vaseline
- Shoes with studs in place
- Rainsheet
- Umbrella (for rider!)
- Grease and gloves
- Towels
- Stud kit
- Ice boots
- Spares
- Bridle
- Overgirth
- Over-reach boots
- Boots and bandages
- Girth
- Martingale
- Breastplate
- Studs
- Gloves for rider

After-Care for Horses

The horse returns to the ten-minute box when he has completed Phase D (the cross-country). Again, the horse's temperature and respiration rate are taken, and you can loosen the noseband, girth, etc. Getting the horse's temperature and respiration back to normal as soon as possible is the priority.

Removing the tack, boots, and bandages speedily is extremely important. Have a quick check to see if there are any injuries so you are aware of what needs to be done when the horse has cooled down.

The fastest way to cool a horse down is to apply lots of icy cold water over his neck and back, but make sure you remove it as soon as possible as it warms very quickly. Keep the horse moving while you are cooling him as this helps with the dispersion of lactic acid. On a hot/warm day cooling with icy water for the first five to ten minutes is advisable, and then change to room-temperature water.

All this time make sure you keep the horse moving!

If you have ice boots these can be put on as soon as possible. A good alternative is to wrap pre-soaked iced Fybagee, but this needs to be changed regularly as leaving warm wraps on the horse's legs is more detrimental than nothing at all.

Once you think your horse is comfortable and you have clearance from the vet, you may leave the ten-minute box. Keeping the horse quietly moving is the best thing you can do, so once you have given him a wash, changed his ice boots and rugged up, take him for a pick of grass so he is not standing still in a confined area. Allowing the horse to have a moderate drink of water periodically is acceptable as re-hydration is very important. However, avoid letting the horse consume a large amount of water and then stand still as this can lead to colic.

Horse Injuries

Many injuries can occur while going cross-country. The most common injury would be bruising, from catching either a knee or stifle on a fence. Cold hosing for the initial ten to twenty minutes is recommended and then, if necessary, alternating cold and heat. This helps with circulation so that haematomas are kept to a minimum. Minor scratches and abrasions can have an anti-bacterial wash applied followed by an antiseptic powder/cream.

Trauma to a joint or tendon is also treated with cold hosing initially to keep swelling to a minimum. The horse's welfare is paramount so if he is showing signs

Here a horse is being prepared for the cross-country phase of the endurance test during the ten-minute halt.

One person has been allocated 'holding duties' while another is splashing down excess sweat with a sponge and water. Extra buckets of water that have been prepared earlier are on hand if needed. The saddle is protected from becoming wet by a towel.

The surcingle and the girth have been loosened and will be tightened again with plenty of time to spare before the rider remounts. The saddle placement will be checked to make sure that it has not moved back.

I wouldn't normally remove the bridle, as has been done here, but would put a headcollar over the top instead. Time is limited and replacing the bridle can sometimes prove difficult if the horse becomes a little fractious. This horse may have needed to have his bridle altered or his bit or noseband changed.

of distress or pain, do not hesitate to contact the vet. By discussing the horse's injury with the vet, you can make a plan as to which treatment will best suit the injury.

Being prepared for injuries and having the correct treatments on hand is very important. You should always carry a veterinary kit of some sort whether you are at a one-day or three-day event.

An Animalintex poultice is very handy as it can be used as either a hot or cold poultice. If need be, it can also be frozen to create an ice pack.

Tubigrip is excellent as you can pack it with ice, placing a layer of Tubigrip on the horse's leg first so you don't cause ice burn. It can be purchased from your pharmacy/chemist.

Arnica cream should never be left at home! It is very good for helping alleviate bruising, but remember never to apply it to open wounds. I tend to feed arnica tablets to my horses before each competition as a preventative measure for bruising.

Whirlpool boots are a good investment. Make sure you get the horse used to them at home before putting him in them at an event.

Physiotherapy is also a consideration and a qualified therapist can do a lot to make the horse feel more comfortable and have it show jump to the best of its ability.

I always apply Uptite (cold kaolin clay) to all the legs once the horse has fully cooled down and after I have seen the horse jog up sound. This helps to draw any heat out of the legs and relieve strains. Use disposable gloves to apply it and don't be afraid to put plenty on, all around the leg and not just on the tendons. Then cover with damp brown paper to help keep the poultice moist for longer, and finally finish with a good wide stable bandage.

Veterinary kit

- Animalintex
- Antiseptic powder
- Arnica cream
- Arnica pills and cream
- Gamgee
- Bandages
- Aloe vera gel
- Tubigrip

Part 3

Analysis of Cross-Country Fence Technique

Uprights

Key points
Approach with balance and control.
Retain engagement.
Allow the fence to come to you, and sit up.

■ IDEAL TECHNIQUE

Fences of an upright nature, such as gates, post and rails, stiles and walls, should be approached with **balance**, **connection** and a certain amount of **control**.

They should not be taken with too much speed and need to be treated with respect.

Because of the unforgiving vertical profile of the fence (especially if there is no obvious ground-line to assist the horse), the rider should endeavour to maintain **engagement** of the horse's stride right up to the jump itself. A sloping fence such as a triple bar will allow some leniency in the accuracy of take-off. A less 'user friendly' upright will not.

Loose reins and a long, strung-out stride should be avoided.

I often explain to my students that when jumping these types of fences they should establish the required controlled, connected stride in plenty of time before the fence. They should then allow the fence to 'come to them'. It will arrive! This will discourage any sense of last-minute urgency and prevent any resistance from the horse in the final strides of his approach.

It is worth remembering that the **connection** should be created by riding the back end of the horse forward into a controlling hand, not by pulling the front end backwards and thereby destroying the forward way of riding. Do not drop the horse's balance in front of the fence, and sit up.

■ PHOTO ANALYSIS

Example 1

Photo 1a In the stride before take-off at this upright gate it is evident that the approach has been good. The horse is on a lovely elastic contact, showing no resistance; his rider's elbows are nicely bent.

The speed has not been too fast, and the engagement is good. There is an obvious spring-like quality to the horse's frame and stride. The rider is in close contact with the saddle, with his shoulders up to encourage a shift in the centre of balance towards the horse's hindquarters

Photo 1b Ideally the take-off could have been a little

closer, but because the horse is well connected the jump is clean and safe with plenty of height.

Example 2

Photo 2a This is a very difficult upright fence with no ground rail, and further complicated by the construction overhead on the approach.

The expression of the rider, and the fact that she has dropped her eyes to the bottom of the fence, could indicate that she is unhappy with the approach. She appears to be coming in a little too fast and a bit deep to the fence, as she is helping the horse to back off with her reins.

Photo 2b Her last-minute adjustments seem to have been successful as the picture is now more confident. The rider has stayed close to the saddle to ensure security and has not got ahead of the movement. By keeping her shoulders well up and her legs nicely forward she has put herself in a good position to stay on if the horse had hit the fence.

Spread Fences

Key points

Ride with impulsion and boldness.
Slightly lengthen the stride in the approach.
Keep the horse in front of your leg.

■ IDEAL TECHNIQUE

A spread fence should be approached on a **powerful** yet slightly **increasing** stride.

On the approach to a vertical fence, the rider will maintain a condensed and regular stride pattern right until the point of take-off, allowing the fence to come to them; whereas to a spread fence, the frame of the horse and the stride he takes should begin to extend. This will enable the jump to be executed with boldness and increased power. There should, however, be no obvious break to the rhythm when lengthening the stride on the approach. The rider should not suddenly accelerate or fire the horse towards the fence. With the increased impulsion created by the rider, the jump should **flow** smoothly from take-off to landing There should be no hovering or dwelling over the fence. In other words, the horse should cope easily with the extra width to the back of the obstacle, thanks to the **scope** created in him by his rider.

The stride should be quietly **lengthening** but should never be completely **lengthened** to the extent where the horse has lost all engagement and the rider lost all accuracy. **Engagement** (connection) and plenty of **impulsion** (contained energy) are still required to create a powerful jump.

Most spread fences tend to ride more easily than uprights as they offer more substance to fill the horse and rider's eye, and they tend to encourage more forward, attacking riding.

The take-off spot should not be too deep to spread fences. Allowing a little more room for the horse in front of the fence will encourage a better forward flow. This take-off spot should be created by producing the correct canter (powerful, forward and increasing) and not by pulling the horse back from the fence. Whenever I have an awkward jump at a spread fence or miss my take-off badly, I know it is always the result of failing to follow these basic principles and not because I have failed to 'see a stride'.

■ PHOTO ANALYSIS

Example 1

Photo 1a Here we have an excellent approach. Both horse and rider look concentrated and confident. They have arrived at the fence on a good forward powerful stride, producing an ideal take-off spot. The rider sits lightly in the saddle and has the horse in front of his leg aids. The horse has his head and neck nicely extended and yet still maintains an elastic contact with the rider's hands.

Photo 1b The impulsion and engagement has ensured sufficient power to create a bold jump.

Photo 1c The forward flow has been maintained throughout and …

Photo 1d …the horse has landed effortlessly about the same distance away from the fence as it had taken off. The rider has his shoulders well up and will land softly into his stirrups.

Example 2

Photo 2a A novice horse and rider tackling a square oxer. It is evident from this photo, taken in the last few strides before the fence, that the horse is not increasing his stride in the approach. The rider is steadying the horse at the last moment and he is resisting her hands. Maybe the approach has been too fast and a last-minute adjustment has taken place to reduce the speed and engage the stride.

Photo 2b As a result the take-off spot is far too close and the horse has hit the front of the fence.

The rider could have adopted a more defensive position when aware that all was not well, by raising her shoulders and sitting behind the centre of balance, and slipping her reins to give the horse more freedom to extricate himself from trouble.

Photo 2c The horse has saved the day with an act of athleticism, but it has to be said that the rider is not in a position to support her horse if he stumbles on landing. With her shoulders forward, her heel up and her lower leg sliding back, she could be in trouble.

Simple Log

Key points
Jumped with the minimum of fuss.
Taken out of the stride and rhythm.
Medium pace and stride pattern.

■ IDEAL TECHNIQUE

Fences that offer a well-defined ground-line and a 'user friendly' profile, such as a simple log, roll-top fence, hay bales, etc. – should be taken with the **minimum of fuss**.

They should be jumped out of the horse's stride and natural rhythm, giving him a confident and enjoyable experience. There should be no messing about in front of the fence by the rider, forcing an alteration to the stride pattern or disrupting the flow. Therefore the rider should ensure that the horse is already moving forward in an **engaged** manner that will enable the fence to be taken **out of his stride**. If the stride is too strung out and disconnected this will be difficult to achieve. The 'spring' of the horse should remain partially 'coiled' throughout to allow the rider some flexibility to make a subtle adjustment to the length of stride, where required. The energy level should be such that the rider feels the fence has simply passed beneath them and did not require any additional effort from the horse. If a rider

wastes just one second in the approach to each of these fences throughout a course, struggling to gain control or reorganising to 'find a stride', then, without even considering the speed at which he is travelling, he is likely to accumulate unnecessary time faults.

▪ PHOTO ANALYSIS

Photo 1 Here the horse and rider have arrived at this simple log fence on an ideal stride and in good balance. The flow to the gallop is uninterrupted and the horse's 'spring' appears to have remained partially 'coiled' throughout. The rider sits close to the saddle without losing the security of the lower leg, which is encouraging forward momentum.

Photo 2 The horse has sighted the fence well and makes his jump with the minimum of fuss. The jump has simply become part of his galloping stride. Unfortunately the rider appears to be over-participating in the jumping effort himself and has risen up a little too high, getting slightly ahead of the horse. This may be acceptable if nothing goes wrong, but could be a concern if it does.

Photo 3 The bascule is completed. I would prefer to see the rider with more weight down into his stirrup as he still appears to be a fraction above the horse and a little too forward. Nevertheless, a good effort and a good result.

Hanging Log

Key points
Approach with a connected stride.
Retain a consistent rhythm.
Engagement of hindquarters.

■ IDEAL TECHNIQUE

The difference between a hanging log and a log resting on the ground is that the hanging log offers no obviously defined ground-line for the horse to sight. Hanging logs remain solid fences that require respect – while they are generally kind on the horse to jump, they can often have considerable 'daylight' between the bottom of the log and the ground.

The rider must therefore take responsibility for ensuring that the stride is a little more **connected** in the approach to the hanging log than is required to take a filled-in simple log.

It is still desirable to take the hanging log out of a consistent **rhythm** and stride pattern, but more accuracy is needed to bring the horse to a comfortable take-off distance to avoid standing off from the fence or running underneath it. As usual, this take-off spot will not be created by reliance on the rider's eye alone, but will be achieved by engaging the horse more. If the stride pattern is condensed then the chances of accuracy are increased.

■ PHOTO ANALYSIS

Photo 1 In this approach it would appear that the desired engagement is missing. The stride is too long. The rider is aware of this and has resorted to driving the horse forward with her seat. (Not as effective as the legs.) Her hands are too high and the horse is beginning to resist; he is backing off the fence instead of going forward.

Photo 2 The jump is made more difficult by the undulating ground on the approach, but it is evident that the horse has stood off much too far from the fence. The rider, however, is allowing him freedom with her reins.

Photo 3 By sitting up in a defensive position and slipping her reins effectively, the rider has diverted possible disaster. She has been quick-thinking and fast-reacting in an awkward situation.

Ditches (see also page 108)

Key points

Approach on a lengthening stride with lots of impulsion.

Rider must keep eyes up and not look down into the ditch.

Ditches require confidence and boldness.

■ IDEAL TECHNIQUE

Ditches are spread fences and as such should be approached on a **lengthening** stride with plenty of **impulsion**. The closer the horse gets to the ditch, the more powerful he should become. The stride should not be reducing, the revs dwindling nor the horse backing off.

Both horse and rider should **not look down**. Looking down will cause the fence to appear to grow in size. Instead the rider should keep his eyes up and simply treat the fence as he would a straightforward triple bar. He should feel that he is travelling 'uphill' and that the horse is not strung out or on a loose rein.

Careful early education and gradual introduction to small ditches will pay dividends throughout the horse's later career. He must learn not to fear ditches but should instead trust his rider and respond to the aids.

Perhaps a lead from another horse may initially be needed to build confidence, but always the impulsion should be building towards the jump, even if in trot.

Ditch and Palisade

■ PHOTO ANALYSIS

Example 1

Photo 1a A ditch and palisade should be met on a lengthening stride as if jumping an ordinary triple bar. The rider should not look down into the ditch but should look up.

Here the rider is endeavouring to generate some power and impulsion, but it would appear that the horse is not responding. His expression does not look forward-thinking and the balance looks a bit downhill. Perhaps the stride is just too long?

Photo 1b Horse and rider are both looking down. The horse is not in front of the rider's leg, as her heel is up, and the balance is too much focused on the forehand.

Photo 1c As a result the jump is made a bit 'low' with the possibility of the horse hitting the fence with his front legs. The rider has needed to play 'catch up' as she was previously too far behind the centre of balance in the approach.

Example 2

Photo 2a Standing off a wide ditch and palisade. The rider has sacrificed accuracy here but has ensured that she has plenty of determination and power. She has probably met the fence on a lengthening stride but has not lost contact with the horse's mouth so the impression is one of going uphill. The rider's eyes are definitely looking up, although she is jumping out of the saddle too much for safety.

Photo 2b They sail over the fence with plenty of height but the rider is a bit loose in her position. She has slipped her reins effectively to allow the horse to stretch the extra distance needed due to standing off the fence. Possibly the whole approach was too fast.

Example 3

Photo 3a Some ditches can be quite deep and wide. With progressive training the horse will develop confidence with ditches and trust his rider. This horse began his career somewhat cautiously where ditches were concerned but here it is evident that he has responded well to my aids. By building extra impulsion into the gallop then increasing the length of his stride the horse knows what lies ahead. He is committed to my commands and to boldness.

Photo 3b Even though the horse has reached the back of this wide fence he still gives the impression of going uphill. My position is slightly 'defensive'.

2b

2a

3b

3a

Trakehner

■ PHOTO ANALYSIS

Photo 1 A confident picture of horse and rider negotiating a trakehner fence. The jump is with plenty of power and without hesitation, and it appears that the ditch below the log has had no affect on the horse. The log suspended above the ditch will tend to help the horse gain height over the fence and present the rider with something to ride boldly towards.

Photo 2 Midway over the fence the confidence and fluency are still evident. The rider's stirrup may be a little too long for cross-country riding.

Photo 3 More bend in the knee would give added security to the rider to enable her to better absorb the impact of landing. Her shoulders are back nicely, the horse is landing well out from the fence and the overall picture is a happy one.

Steps Up

▪ Key points

Plenty of power and impulsion.

Retain engagement to create a bouncy stride.

Look up and stay in balance with weight in the stirrups.

▪ IDEAL TECHNIQUE

Steps up require plenty of **power** and **impulsion** from the horse.

The energy level must remain strong throughout the sequence of efforts to ensure that the horse is still moving positively forwards once it has reached the top. Bouncing up a succession of large steps takes a fair amount of physical effort.

As the face of the steps are upright in their profile, the stride should be held together to create a bouncy, powerful approach. It is not desirable to be strung out or too fast. It is engagement and controlled power at a medium pace that will allow the rider accuracy to the first step. If the first step is jumped badly then the rest will follow suit.

The rider should stay light with his seat, with his weight on his stirrups, to allow the horse the freedom to make his numerous jumping efforts. Sitting heavily in the saddle should be avoided. If sitting light, the power must be generated from the rider's legs, so they should remain active. Eyes should be looking up where the rider intends to go, not looking down into the bottom of each step. The former will promote positive riding from start to finish. An elastic contact should be maintained at all times to prevent the horse from becoming disconnected. Loose reins will allow the spring to uncoil.

▪ PHOTO ANALYSIS

Example 1

Photo 1a Here we have a novice level question of two steps up with a bounce between each element.

This horse, which could well be inexperienced, seems a little suspicious of the second bank.

From the rider's obvious urging it could be guessed that the impulsion was lacking and there is a danger of the energy level running low. The stride in the approach may

have been too long and as a result the jump has lacked height. The rider is beginning to get caught behind the movement and does not have his leg underneath his bodyweight for support of his own balance.

Photo 1b Determination on the rider's part has ensured a successful ascent. However, he is in need of his reins too much for his own balance, and the horse, with shortened neck, appears to be losing further impulsion.

Photo 1c Still climbing uphill and approaching the next fence the rider is aware that the steps have impeded the forward progress so he is adopting strong tactics to get back on track. Across country there is only one opportunity

to negotiate each fence without incurring penalties, so recovering quickly from a mistake and forward thinking is essential.

Example 2

Photo 2a An excellent approach to steps up. Both horse and rider are looking up and the spring is well coiled to give an impression of plenty of impulsion and power. The rider's weight is well distributed over the centre of balance, with her seat light. The horse is placing his hocks well underneath him to generate plenty of 'push'.

Photo 2b At the second step there has been no loss of power or energy. The rider has allowed the reins to slip through her hands, and as a result has needed to let her elbows come out to compensate for the extra length. She has, however, maintained her own independence of balance on her stirrup, and has not lost the engagement.

Photo 2c Even at the top of the rise after the steps the horse is still taking the rider forward as a result of having not lost any impulsion. The rider needs to get forward again and re-shorten her reins.

Steps Down

Key points

Approach with control and balance.
Not too fast.
Don't get ahead of the movement.

◼ IDEAL TECHNIQUE

Where steps up require power, impulsion and bold riding, steps down require the opposite. Steps down demand **control** and **balance**.

The approach should not be too fast, so that the horse is allowed the opportunity to digest the problem ahead before proceeding down it with confidence.

Approaching too fast may cause the horse to become concerned, encouraging him to think backwards at the last minute. An inexperienced horse may even benefit initially from a few steps of trot before the first element, but, once he is confident, a steady, well-connected canter stride can be adopted to maintain forward and positive jumping.

Although the landing will influence the approach, there is no point in being ready for the descent if you fail to take off, so an encouraging leg should be applied to prevent a refusal. The jump will be easier to sit to if it is fluent and positive.

It is very important that the rider does not get ahead of the movement at any stage, so he must not lean too far forward and should take the impact of each landing on the stirrups and not on his knees or seat. It would be preferable for the rider to be slightly behind the movement in this instance than ahead of it; and it may be necessary to slip the reins a little to allow the horse some freedom to make his descent.

◼ PHOTO ANALYSIS

Example 1

Photo 1a An advanced sequence of steps down. Here the rider has somewhat exaggerated the point of not getting caught ahead of the movement, to the extent that she has failed to keep the horse in front of her leg. Her upper body is behind her base support, her lower leg. The descent is very steep as a result of the horse not being forward enough, and without fluency it will be difficult to sit the jump. The rider has slipped her reins to allow the horse freedom, but so much so that she has lost the control. It would be better if she had kept her hands lower, as she has broken the ideal line from elbow to bit (indicating loss of control).

Photo 1b The horse has failed to bounce on down the next step and as a result the rider has been pitched forward dramatically. At this point she is in a precarious position and is unable to ride the horse forward. She is looking down, and

her contact with the horse's mouth is non-existent.

Photo 1c The process of regaining balance and control has begun. The rider is quickly gathering up her reins. She is now looking ahead, and she is endeavouring to get back over the centre of her horse's balance.

Photo 1d An altogether better picture. The rider's weight is now well centred over the horse. Her shoulders are up and back, but this is not over-done, and while her rein contact is long, the connection and control are not abandoned. A remarkable recovery.

Example 2

Photo 2a Here it is very probable that because of the closeness of the preceding fence to the steps the rider has arrived at this point much faster than she would like. She is already making a correction with the left rein to the straightness of her descent, and she has lifted her shoulders to ensure that she does not get ahead of the movement.

Photo 2b A mistake occurs as a result of the lack of control and preparation.

Photo 2c The rider shows great 'stickability' and balance, and remains in the saddle. She has never failed to keep her eyes up, nor has she completely lost contact with her horse's mouth. She has ensured her own independent balance by keeping her leg underneath her at all times.

Corner

Key points

Know your line – where you plan to jump and the
line needed to get there.
A straight approach going forward.
Engaged stride with lots of impulsion.

■ IDEAL TECHNIQUE

Corner fences are a test of the horse's **straightness** and of
the rider's **accuracy** and **control**.

The correct line of approach must first be established by
careful study and walking of the fence. The presentation
should then be made at a medium pace with a **powerful** yet
connected stride.

The correct line of approach would generally be perpen-
dicular to an imaginary line that bisects the two rails of the
corner. This may require holding a line on an angle to the
face of the fence. Some corners open up very wide close to
the apex, but the rider should avoid galloping in on a long
strung-out stride as this will allow the horse the opportunity
to run out at the last minute through the rider being inaccurate or lacking control.

Instead, the rider should keep the stride partially connected to bring the horse close to the base of the fence, and
to channel the horse straight between his legs and hands.
Plenty of impulsion will be needed to allow the jump to
occur easily within the rhythm. The pace should not be so
slow that the jump requires an additional huge effort from
the horse on take-off.

To ride straight it is best to ride forward, so the rider
should establish the controlled stride pattern early in the
approach and then continue riding quietly forward near the
fence. Pulling against the horse or riding 'backwards' will
promote crookedness.

■ PHOTO ANALYSIS

Example 1

Photo 1a Here we see a good approach towards a corner
fence. Although several strides still remain before the jump,
the horse and rider are already organised. The stride is well
engaged, not too long, and the horse is nicely on the rider's
aids. The control is evident by the good bend in the rider's
elbows. Both are well focused on the fence itself.

Photo 1b The last stride before take-off, and no engagement or control has been lost. The rider still has the horse
in 'front' of his leg and supported in his hand, and he is sitting up well. He has not toppled forward and there is no
slackness in the reins.

Photo 1c Keeping the stride engaged has brought the
horse close to the base of the fence. There is no chance of
a last-minute run-out.

Photo 1d Absolute straightness is maintained throughout
the jump, and the horse displays sufficient power to allow
the back rail of the fence to pass beneath him easily.

Example 2

Photo 2a In contrast to the previous example, the approach for this rider doesn't appear to have gone as well as he would have hoped. He is driving hard to lengthen his horse's stride and has already begun to adjust the horse's line by opening his left rein. There is a tiny amount of resistance from the horse.

Photo 2b The pair has arrived at the fence a long way off, and the loose reins and straight elbows of the rider are not desirable. The engagement and impulsion needed are missing. The rider is, however, well centred and obviously very committed.

Photo 2c This time, with a bit of luck, they have got away with it. Given the chance again I am sure that the rider would choose to engage the stride more to ensure better control and accuracy.

Fence on an Upward Slope

Key points

Plenty of power with an engaged stride.

Retain the forward impulsion.

Sit light but with an active leg.

■ IDEAL TECHNIQUE

Riding a fence at the top of an upward slope is a relatively straightforward exercise providing that the horse is **engaged** and possesses plenty of **power**.

The horse will already be propelling himself forward to negotiate the rise, with his weight mainly distributed over his 'engine', or hindquarters. This will put him in a better balance to make the jump occur more easily than if he were going downhill on his forehand.

It will be more difficult, however, for the rider to judge his stride or distance to the fence than when on flat ground. He must rely instead on finding a good point of take-off by flowing forward and retaining the connection of the horse to achieve accuracy. This connection will give the horse the power and spring necessary to jump out of his stride, even if it means standing off from the fence. If the horse is not too strung out he should not come up underneath the fence and he could quickly shuffle an extra stride if urgently needed.

The power and impulsion must be generated by the rider's legs. Sitting heavily in the saddle and pushing the horse forward with the seat will not help. Rather it will impede the horse's progress.

■ PHOTO ANALYSIS

Photo 1 At the base of the slope the rider is generating plenty of impulsion. She has the horse moving positively forward and yet she has not lost the connection of stride or 'spring'.

Both horse and rider are looking towards the top of the slope, which is where they need to go.

Photo 2 Still the rider is driving with her legs to ensure no loss of power and she retains some engagement. She has a good line between her elbow and the horse's mouth, and although she sits close to the saddle her weight is mainly in the stirrup.

Photo 3 It is evident in this photo that no energy has been lost. The horse is still taking the rider to the fence, despite the steep rise.

Photo 4 There has been no alteration to the rhythm from the bottom of the slope to the top, nor has there been any alteration to the length of stride. The rider has not relied exclusively on her eye to bring her to the fence on a suitable distance but has made the jump fit into her stride pattern. The horse is showing an extraordinary degree of engagement, with his back legs coming well underneath his bodyweight to execute his jump.

Photo 5 The jump is made with ease, directly out of the stride and rhythm.

Fence on a Downward Slope

Key points

Do not allow the horse onto his forehand.

Slow, engaged approach with the hindquarters well underneath the horse.

Sit up.

■ IDEAL TECHNIQUE

It is generally more difficult to jump a fence going downhill than one that is uphill. The horse will not be in a good natural balance so the rider must assist him to prevent him from falling onto his forehand as he descends the slope. It is awkward for a horse to make his jump off his forehand so he will need the rider's **support** to keep his hocks underneath him.

The stride should be well **engaged** to prevent the horse from running underneath the fence or standing too far off. The speed should be **controlled**, not too fast, and the stride should not be 'strung out'.

The rider must keep his shoulders well up so that his weight is centred towards the horse's hindquarters. He should not lose the rein contact and **drop** the horse in the approach.

▪ PHOTO ANALYSIS

Photo 1 At the top of the downward slope to this upright log the horse already appears too strung out. His nose is well out in front and the rider's reins are too long to offer any support to his balance or to the engagement of his stride. The horse may have lost momentum and confidence earlier as the rider appears to be driving him on. However, it appears that she is using a lot of seat, as her leg is ahead of her weight and she is not getting the response that she desires.

Photo 2 The horse is now completely on his forehand, so making a jump from his hindquarters will be difficult. His frame is too long and the engagement is gone.

Photo 3 His best option is to stand right off the fence or he risks hitting the fence hard if he takes another stride.

Photo 4 The task is too difficult and he catches his back legs on the fence. The rider has taken evasive action well, and she sits right back, giving the horse plenty of rein. A shorter, more engaged stride, with the balance more focused on the horse's hindquarters would have produced a better result.

Coffin

Key points
A slow, controlled approach.
Keep horse in front of the leg with lots of impulsion.
Rider must keep shoulders up in the approach.

IDEAL TECHNIQUE

The approach to a coffin fence should be made in a **controlled** canter but with plenty of **power** and **impulsion** (contained energy). Coffins are one of the more difficult types of cross-country fence, so the horse must be given time to assess the technicalities ahead and should be presented without too much speed. To avoid the potential for a refusal, however, the rider will need to engage the horse's engine and keep up plenty of revs to encourage confidence. **A short, bouncy** canter with plenty of power is ideal.

It is easy for the rider to get ahead of the movement on the way into a coffin, so he must remember to keep his shoulders up and his weight into his stirrups. The horse's eye may well be drawn towards the ditch beyond the rails before he has executed his initial jump, which may cause him to 'rub' the rails with his forelegs or entangle his hind ones. This will especially be the case if the approach has been too fast. The rider should not drop his horse onto the shoulders but should support the forehand well, keeping the hocks right up underneath the horse. By maintaining a connected stride in the approach to the rails, the take-off should be ideal. It is only when the stride is too strung out that the horse will get underneath the fence or stand way off, which for coffins is undesirable.

The three elements of a coffin must be ridden as a combination, and once over the first element the rider's responsibilities are not complete. He must keep his eyes up on the exit and not look down into the ditch. He needs to encourage the horse forward with his legs, stay light in the saddle for the uphill approach to the last element, and retain the impulsion and connection needed for a clean jump.

If possible, a straight line should be ridden throughout. It is not a good idea to take a coffin on an angle as this can lead to an unseated rider or a horse fall.

PHOTO ANALYSIS

Example 1

Photo 2 Here is a good approach to the first element of a novice coffin. The rider is sitting up well with her upper body to prevent getting caught ahead of the movement should anything go wrong during the jump. Her eyes are looking up and she has good engagement of her horse, with nicely bent elbows and a secure contact through her reins. The horse's attention is already on the ditch that follows and yet he has fully comprehended the immediate problem as the approach has not been hurried.

Photo 3 The jump is cleanly executed. The rider still has an elastic contact with the horse's mouth. From this point she will raise her shoulders to remain over the horse's centre of balance.

Photo 4 Despite the confident jump the horse is a little suspicious of the downhill landing and ditch so has jumped a fraction crooked over the rails. The rider has always been looking ahead so reacts with subtlety to straighten him. She remains over the centre of balance and still displays a good

line from her elbow to the horse's bit, indicating that she has not lost the connection. Her bent elbows show that there is no restriction or resistance.

Photo 5 Horse and rider make a positive jump over the ditch and are already preparing for the final element.

Photo 6 Coming up the slope to the rails the rider is light with her seat and is again forward with her upper body to remain with the movement. She encourages the horse forward with her leg but for the first time she has lost the elasticity in her arms by raising her hands a fraction ...

Photo 7 ... so the horse remains a little high in his head and neck during the jump even though the contact is now a bit loose. Otherwise his form is excellent with his knees well up.

Coffin

Example 2

Photo 1 Here we see an approach that is less good. The rider is well behind the centre of the horse's balance and drives with his seat and legs at the same time as he fights for control. There appears to have been too much speed and the horse is resisting the rider. The horse's head is up and he does not seem to be focused on the fence at all.

Photo 2 At the last minute the horse needs to put his 'brakes' on as he suddenly sees the ditch beyond the rails. The rider has done a good job to remain close to the saddle with his shoulders well up and so has avoided toppling forward as the momentum is checked. He has not given up and continues to encourage the horse forward.

Photo 3 The horse loses his jumping technique and tips over his forehand because he has not had time to prepare well for the rails. He has not been impeded in his efforts of self-preservation by his rider, who stays independently balanced and gives the horse as much rein as is required.

Photo 4 A strong and determined ride has ensured that forward progress is maintained, but because of the speed a severe correction is required to remedy the sideways movement as the horse reacts to the ditch. Consequently the horse's expression does still not indicate forward-thinking.

Photo 5 An awkward jump over the ditch follows.

Photo 6 With all that has gone on previously, the last element has produced a risky jump. The horse has dived at the rails, hitting the top with his foreleg. Throughout the entire sequence the rider has never been caught ahead of the movement, and so although it has not been very pretty, he has succeeded in negotiating the obstacle.

Bullfinch/Hedge

Key points

Rhythm maintained throughout.
Medium stride and pace.
Rider to sit up and keep lower leg forward.

■ IDEAL TECHNIQUE

A bullfinch, brush or hedge does not pose a lot of technical questions but asks for boldness and trust from the horse. These fences should be taken out of the **rhythm** of the gallop at a **medium pace** and from a **medium length of stride**. Some engagement must be maintained to ensure that there is no last-minute alteration to the stride pattern. These fences should give the horse a confident experience and, with mileage, the horse will become accustomed to brushing through the top of them. Initially he may try to jump right over the top, so the rider should be prepared to sit back and slip the reins if needed.

If the construction of the fence consists of tall, strong brush then there may need to be a reduction in the speed and the stride may need to be shortened. The rider should sit well up and not let his lower leg be dragged back behind him, spoiling his security on landing.

■ PHOTO ANALYSIS

Photo 1 The approach to this bullfinch hedge has been made at a good gallop. The stride is of medium pace and length so the horse is able to make his jump out of his rhythm with the minimum of fuss. The rider sits up nicely in anticipation of a big jump and supports the horse between his legs and hands.

Photo 2 The jump begins from a comfortable distance at take-off appropriate to the speed and stride. The rhythm is uninterrupted.

Photo 3 The jump looks clean and confident.

Photo 4 The landing is well out from the fence, with plenty of scope, and the whole jump has been fluent throughout. The tall parts of the bullfinch may have dragged the rider's lower leg back during the jump, so he is in danger of taking the landing on his knee unless he quickly reacts. His shoulders are well up to counteract this problem.

Bank Up Followed by Fence

Key points

Rider must keep a light seat with weight in the stirrup and eyes looking up.

Powerful yet controlled stride with plenty of engagement.

Must keep riding forward, especially after jumping onto the bank.

▪ IDEAL TECHNIQUE

A bank up to a fence on top should be ridden as a combination. There should be a flowing rhythm throughout.

The approach to the bank should be **powerful** yet the stride should contain the necessary **engagement** to ensure that the 'spring' of the horse is coiled sufficiently to create a positive jump.

The approach strides should not be strung out or too fast, as the rider will lose accuracy to the upright face of the bank.

The rider should be **looking up**, towards the jump on the top, not looking down into the bottom of the bank. This will encourage forward riding.

The rider's weight should be light, with the support in the stirrup; the rider should not sit heavily in the saddle. As usual the **impulsion** should be generated by the rider's legs.

Once on top of the bank the horse's first stride will normally be shortened so the rider must continue to ride forward immediately. The degree of success achieved at the following jump will be decided by how well the rider maintains the energy level between the jumping efforts. The approach strides to the jump on top should not be unduly affected by the preceding bank.

Bank, One Stride to Palisade

▪ PHOTO ANALYSIS

Photo 1 Horse and rider make their jump up the bank. The rider is in a good position, with her balance on her stirrups, her seat light and her eyes looking ahead. The horse appears to be losing power, so the approach may have been a little lacking in impulsion. He is drifting a little to the left.

Photo 2 The horse now has his head too high, indicating a loss of momentum. The rider corrects the crookedness but is temporarily unbalanced with too much weight in the saddle, and she is supported too much by her reins.

Photo 3 The rider remembers to ride the distance between the two jumping efforts positively and has again come light in her seat. The horse is responding nicely to her leg and is building impulsion towards the next fence.

Photo 4 The jump is negotiated safely but the rider is too high above the horse. She has jumped up over the fence herself!

Bank to Narrow Brush

■ PHOTO ANALYSIS

Photo 1 A positive approach to a step up followed by a narrow brush. Both horse and rider are looking up and there is an excellent line between the rider's elbow and the horse's bit, indicating good engagement. The rider may be pivoting on her knee too much, which doesn't allow the weight to be fully down into her heel.

Photo 2 The horse is still nicely engaged at the point of take-off. His hind legs are coming well through, and the rider offers support with a good, elastic contact.

Photo 3 For some reason the landing is awkward (lack of impulsion possibly) and a stumble occurs. However, the rider has never stopped looking ahead and has not lost the contact with the horse.

Photo 4 Quick reactions ensure that the momentum is restored immediately, and although the rider drives forward hard she does not lose the engagement.

Photo 5 The rider has held her line and achieves a good presentation to the final element.

Upright Followed by Bank Down

Key points

Approach with engagement and reduced speed.
Ensure impulsion.
Keep shoulders up.

■ IDEAL TECHNIQUE

When negotiating an upright fence that immediately precedes a bank or drop down, what lies behind the upright will influence the approach. The drop may suddenly alarm the horse or draw his attention away from the upright itself, so care must be taken to approach with maximum **engagement** and at a **reduced speed**.

Failure to ensure **impulsion**, however, could result in a last-minute refusal, so the rider should remember to keep his leg on strongly.

There should be no late, hasty corrections in front of the fence to cause resistance or to distract the horse's attention, and the stride should remain constant all the way up to the fence. The rider should not 'throw' the horse at the fence, stand off, or break the rhythm.

As would be the case when jumping into a coffin-type fence, the rider should keep his **shoulders up** and his seat close to the saddle to avoid being caught ahead of the

movement. Once over the rails, the rider's leg should be applied to encourage the horse to move forward and to jump out confidently from the bank.

PHOTO ANALYSIS

Example 1

Photo 1 As luck would have it, I am showing a good, secure position over an upright fence that immediately precedes a bank drop. My lower leg is offering a good source of security as it remains underneath my upper bodyweight, and my seat is close to the saddle. My shoulders are up and my eyes are looking ahead. The horse's focus is very obviously on the bank ahead, but because he has not been presented with too much pace he is able to execute a clean jump.

Photo 2 My shoulders have remained upright here to prevent getting ahead of the movement and I have begun to slip the reins to allow the horse to prepare for the drop. However, I have not lost the contact, and there is a good line from my elbow to the horse's mouth. The horse appears to be steadying himself but is still making a good, clean jump.

Photo 3 and 4 Throughout the sequence another line is nearly always evident in my position — one that could be drawn between my heel, my hip and my shoulder.

Photo 5 The impact of landing down the drop is taken on the feet, just as I would want it if I had jumped down the bank without my horse. I would not want to land on my knees or seat!

Upright Followed by Bank Down

Example 2

Photo 1 A much less experienced horse and rider combination tackling the same obstacle. Because they have not achieved the same degree of training it would appear that the approach has involved too much speed instead of the required engagement and impulsion. They have arrived at the fence very close. The rider has begun to go too high above his horse.

Photo 2 The horse is now aware of the drop and begins to steady his pace. As a result he loses his form over the fence. The rider is too far forward, but has maintained an elastic contact with the rein, so is not impeding the horse. His weight is still secure in his lower leg and his eyes are ahead.

Photo 3 A moment of hesitation has occurred. If the rider were back a little he would have more chance of encouraging the horse forward.

Photo 4 The final landing is very secure, and the attempt will have been a good learning experience for them both.

Water Fences (see also page 108)

Key points

Controlled approach with reduced speed.

Keep horse in front of the leg with plenty of impulsion.

Sit back to land securely.

■ IDEAL TECHNIQUE

Water fences should be ridden with **controlled impulsion**. They should not be negotiated with excessive speed or a fall could occur when entering the water. The forward momentum of the horse may be checked by the effect that the 'drag' of the water has on the horse's balance, so to land securely the pace should be controlled.

Not all horses will be immediately comfortable with water, so sympathetic and gradual education will be needed to gain their confidence. A solid foundation of trust must be instilled in the horse if he is to jump happily into the uncertain.

First he should be introduced to a shallow water with a

firm base, in either walk or trot. It is often a good idea to have an experienced horse at hand to give him a lead. If the horse can see that his companion is happy and in no difficulty it will give him confidence. He should become accustomed to the splash and noise of the water before he is asked to jump in.

It may take many repetitions of the lesson at different water fences until any suspicions or concerns of the horse disappear, but eventually the rider should feel that the horse will jump unquestioningly into any water to which he is presented, regardless of the type of fence constructed in and around the water itself.

When there is a drop into water, all the rules for drop fences apply (see description of ideal technique for drops, page 84) but extra emphasis on the speed and control will be required.

Travelling through water well becomes very important when there is a jump out, or even a jump in the water itself. Engagement and impulsion will still be needed, regardless of the water. The bank out should be treated as if it were on dry land. The horse should not drop behind the rider's leg or be allowed onto a long rein. As many people fall off coming out of water as going in!

■ PHOTO ANALYSIS

Example 1

Photo 1 A clean landing into water. The entry has not been made too fast, but with controlled power giving a balanced landing. The rider has not got ahead of the movement but has given the horse the necessary freedom without losing the contact. If the horse were to stumble on the next stride the rider would be able to offer him some support.

Photo 2 They move through the water as though it isn't there. The horse hasn't fallen behind the rider's leg nor become strung out and disconnected. The rider is gathering up his reins to ensure control and engagement for the exit.

Photo 3 A clean jump out is made. The rider remains light and his eyes have been ahead at all times.

Photo 4 The stride between the bank and the jump is still powerful and engaged despite the approach through the water. The rider is maintaining the forward progress with his legs and not his seat.

Photo 5 They easily jump the last element of the sequence. Balance and rhythm have been constant throughout. There has been no loss of control through too much pace.

Water Fences

Example 2

Photo 1 The horse in this picture is showing concern about the water ahead. The rider has used her whip in the approach to the fence but the horse is evincing a little reluctance.

Photo 2 The horse stalls in his momentum and lowers himself into the water, giving the logs very little clearance. The rider has kept her shoulders well up and so does not get pitched forward.

Photo 3 The descent has been very steep and there is a large splash as a result. The rider has done an excellent job of maintaining her own balance. She still has a 'feel' on her horse's mouth, despite having both reins in one hand, and she has thrown back her whip hand as a counterbalance to the check in forward flow.

Photo 4 With the loss of power throughout the jump the horse drops to trot on landing. The rider begins to gather her reins and attempts to regenerate the momentum but ...

Photo 5 ... by the time the bank arrives, the engagement is lacking. The horse misses his step and flounders up the exit bank.

Water Fences

Example 3

This water complex is approached on a downhill slope and lies among darkened trees. It is difficult to bring the horse to the jump with balance and confidence.

Photo 1 Here we see the horse backing off too much in the last stride. Possibly the approach has been too fast. The horse should be allowed time to evaluate the situation before being ridden forward. It would be better if the last stride were more positive to allow the jump to be fluent.

Photo 2 Perhaps it has been sheer speed that has got the combination to this point. It appears that the horse is applying his 'brakes' and the rider has been pitched forwards into a precarious position.

Photo 3 Gingerly they are on their way in. The rider is in no position to remain in the saddle if a stumble should occur, but she is allowing the horse to sort himself out of trouble with a loose rein. She catches her own balance on her horse's neck.

1

Water Fences

Example 4

Photo 1 The approach to the log has been made off a lengthening stride due to the spread of the fence. Some loss of control is evident from the length of rein. The approach is also downhill and off a turn, but the rider is committed and shows her experience by sitting up well. She is already making a correction to her line by looking ahead to the next obstacle and turning her shoulders slightly.

Photo 2 The jump has been extravagant and it has been necessary for the rider to slip her reins a lot. The horse has pushed his head and neck well down to balance himself. The rider is displaying good security, with her weight well down into her stirrups, and, despite the horse's efforts, her independence has not been compromised.

Photo 3 The engagement and forward momentum needed for the fence in the water has been lost due to the reins being slipped at the previous fence. The rider drives on strongly to compensate.

Photo 4 A risky jump has occurred, but the rider has shown great self-preservation. She has got well back behind the movement to maximise her chances of staying in the saddle if the horse stumbles.

Photo 5 Trouble averted, the rider wastes no time in putting the incident behind her and kicks on positively to the next fence.

Bounces

Key points

Rider must retain an independent balance with a
light seat.

Controlled, engaged stride with lots of impulsion.

Good connection throughout, keeping the 'spring
coiled'.

■ IDEAL TECHNIQUE

Bounces require maximum **engagement** as well as plenty of
impulsion. They should not be taken too fast or an awkward
jump could occur if the horse lands into the face of the second element. Instead the power must be controlled by the
rider and the stride pattern shortened. This will ensure that
the **connection** is achieved to create the '**spring**' needed
for the horse to stay neat in his bascule. He should not be
long and flat in his stride.

Although the speed is reduced, the impulsion must not
be lost; the energy level must not dwindle throughout the
combination, especially when negotiating a double bounce.

This is when a horse that is in front of the rider's leg will
be appreciated.

The engagement should be achieved by riding the
horse's 'engine' (his back end) up into a supporting hand,
and not by pulling the front end backwards, which will
destroy the rhythm or create resistance.

The rider must retain independence of balance at all
times. He should not topple forward nor drop the horse's
balance in the approach. His weight should be into his lower
leg to generate the power as well as to ensure his own
security, and his seat should be light to allow the horse
complete freedom to manoeuvre. He should remain over
the centre of balance throughout and should not push his
shoulders too far forward or he will risk getting in front of
the movement.

■ PHOTO ANALYSIS

Example 1

Photo 1 With a stride to go before take-off, the rider appears
concerned about her distance and energy. She is driving
positively but has lost a little of the weight into her lower leg
by sitting in the saddle. And the horse is raising his head too
much. (The martingale seems restrictive.)

Photo 2 The stride has been too long and flat and so the
take-off will be too far away. The rider has remained very
determined and has kept the horse 'out in front of her'. She
has not toppled forward nor dropped the contact.

Photo 3 The horse is landing a little short over the first
element of the bounce, although the rider is in a very good,
secure position.

Photo 4 As a result the horse has stood off the second
element and is somewhat 'diving' in his jump. The rider has
needed to push her shoulders forward over the fence to
stay with the flat jump, which will place her ahead of the
movement if a mishap occurs on landing. A determined ride
has been rewarded by success but a more engaged
approach would have been preferable.

Bounces

Example 2

Photo 1 Here the rider is approaching on a forward yet engaged stride. His weight is well centred and the horse is well connected between his leg and hand. There is no resistance from the horse and his hindquarters are well underneath him.

Photo 2 At the point of take-off, the horse's 'spring' is well coiled. His hind legs are still well up underneath him to give him plenty to push off with.

Photo 3 The engagement and impulsion have produced a fluent jump. The rider still has the horse between his leg and hand and he is in an excellent independent balance. He is ready for both the landing and the take-off, as his body-weight is distributed over the horse's centre of balance.

Photo 4 The final element is completed without loss of impulsion. Still the rider is well centred and it is evident from the fact that the rider is already turning to make a quick getaway that there has been no loss of momentum.

Bounces into Water

■ PHOTO ANALYSIS

Photo 1 The approach to this bounce is being made much more strongly than normal as the water and drop are likely to cause the horse to back off and slow down. Here we can see that the rider is less concerned about the engagement of the stride than he is about the power and energy level. He is sitting very well but the slightly straight elbows will have contributed to the loss of elasticity and connection.

Photo 2 The rider is already riding his jump into the water before he has even landed at the previous fence. He has not taken his leg off through the jump as he wants the horse to jump well into the bounce to bring him close up to the next log. There will be no confusion in the horse's mind as to whether he should bounce or shuffle a stride.

Photo 3 All legs are off the ground, but the horse still gives the impression that he is going forward. The rider has slipped his reins in readiness for the drop but by bending his elbows and raising his hands he has maintained the engagement.

Photo 4 The horse begins to jump well out, and although the rider has stayed back nicely his knee is rising up making it necessary to...

Photo 5 ... exaggerate his defensive position on landing in the water. Better to be safe than sorry!

3

4

Hayrack

Key points
Approach should be controlled.
Straight approach – never angle this type of fence.
Engaged stride with impulsion.

■ IDEAL TECHNIQUE

A hayrack is an example of a fence that offers a false ground-line and so therefore is technically demanding. It is easy for the horse to misjudge his own take-off, as he would normally assess his stride by looking to the base of the fence to gauge his distance. The front profile of the fence is not forgiving, so **accuracy** is needed to avoid getting underneath the fence and hitting the top.

The stride on the approach should be well **engaged** and controlled. The rider should not release the 'spring' of the horse and lengthen the stride as would be normal to a spread, but should instead keep the spring half way coiled all the way to the fence – more like negotiating an upright.

Pulling back against the horse should be avoided or resistance may occur. The horse will need to stay focused on the fence.

It would not be advisable to ride too fast to a hayrack and these fences always should be taken straight, never on an angle.

■ PHOTO ANALYSIS

Photo 1 An experienced combination of horse and rider in a competitive situation against the clock.

The approach is being made at considerable speed. The

rider is very aware that unless she takes some preventative measures she will be in danger of running underneath the fence. Although there is some ground-line here, it is not really well defined and the profile of the hayrack is unforgiving. The rider begins to shorten the horse's stride and meets some resistance.

Photo 2 At the last minute there is the desired response as the horse begins to 'back off' the fence and place some weight on his hindquarters. The rider has ended up on a long rein, due to the preceding big fence, but keeps some elasticity in the contact by allowing her elbows to go out.

Photo 3 The rider continues to 'protect' the horse from the front of the fence with her reins and at no time drops the contact completely.

Photo 4 She is rewarded with a speedy but clean jump.

Drop Fences

Key points

Not to be taken with excessive speed.
Slightly increase length of stride before take-off.
Rider must stay back, slipping the reins if necessary.

■ IDEAL TECHNIQUE

Drop fences should not be taken with **excessive speed**. The horse will need time to remain in balance when landing down onto a lower level. Riding too fast may cause the horse to knuckle over or lose his footing.

Instead, the horse should be presented at a medium pace that retains the engagement to provide impulsion. If there is a slight **increase in power** and **length of stride** in front of the fence involving a drop it will encourage the horse to jump out in his descent. This will make the landing more secure and the jump easier for the rider to sit. If the trajectory of landing is too steep it will be more unseating and will increase the chances of the horse toppling over. When the drop simply involves a plain bank down, the approach may be a bit slower to allow the horse to adjust his balance and lower himself down the step.

It is important that the rider does not get ahead of the movement over drop fences, so he should allow his shoulders to become more upright over the fence to keep his bodyweight back. It will be necessary for the rider to 'slip' his reins at this point to enable the horse to have the freedom to stretch his neck downwards to balance himself on landing. The rider should open his fingers and let the horse take as much rein as he requires, rather than abandoning the contact completely, throwing the reins at the horse and risking loss of control.

The rider should take the impact of landing on his feet just as if he had jumped down the drop without his horse. He should not land heavily on his seat or allow his leg to slip

back, causing him to land on his knees. Both of these faults will reduce security and may result in unseating the rider.

▧ PHOTO ANALYSIS

Example 1

Photo 1 A good, unhurried approach to a simple log drop. This mare has been allowed time to assess the problem and it appears from her expression that she is confident. The rider sits well up so as not to get caught ahead of the movement, and she is allowing the horse to take a little rein through her fingers to give her the freedom to stretch her neck. The rider has her leg well on to encourage the horse to jump out.

Photo 2 The horse begins to lower herself down with a precise jump. There has been no fumbling.

Photo 3 The mare lands well out with fluency. Throughout the rider has maintained her own independence of balance through her stirrup, and she has slipped her reins without losing the control.

Photo 4 A secure landing for both horse and rider. The rider has not got ahead of the movement and will take the impact of landing nicely on her feet. She will immediately gather up her reins as she moves off from the jump.

Drop Fences

Example 2

Photo 2a A very bold approach to a palisade fence with a drop, possibly with just a bit too much speed. I do, however, like the rider's elastic elbows and rein contact, showing that she has not 'dropped' the horse or lost the engagement.

Photo 2b The horse has thrown an extravagant leap but as a result of the extra pace has needed to twist his body to get his back end away from hitting the fence. The rider is taking good defensive measures. She has allowed her lower leg to come right forward as a brace, and she has kept her weight well back. She has slipped the rein a fraction but is still trying to slow the speed by retaining a strong contact.

Photo 2c A good recovery. The rider appears in no danger of being unseated although there remains a question mark over the speed of landing. The descent has been quite steep as a result of the twisting, increasing the chances of knuckling over or stumbling.

Example 3

Photo 3a A substantial four-star log with a considerable drop. Here the rider is already sensing a problem. Maybe the approach has been too quick? She is shifting her shoulders back rapidly and has begun to slip the reins to allow the horse to extract himself from possible trouble. He may well 'rub' the fence with his back legs, so the forward momentum could be severely checked.

Photo 3b Knocking the fence behind has thrown the horse's hindquarters high, but the rider has been ready. She is not ahead of the movement and has allowed the horse to stretch his neck. Her lower leg has slipped back a little so she will take the impact of landing on her knees instead of her feet.

Photo 3c An anxious moment in the next stride. Although the rider is now being pitched forward she has sat the landing and so is in with a chance of recovery. Success would be enhanced by looking up and by a better base support below the knee. Horses will nearly always attempt to correct their own balance if they are not impeded by their rider, and as this rider has allowed the horse complete freedom and has 'stickability' they gallop on to the next fence.

Arrowhead

Key points

Controlled and engaged stride.

Horse must be straight.

Rider must remain upright with the horse between
leg and hand.

■ IDEAL TECHNIQUE

Like corner fences and angled approaches, arrowheads are
a test of **accuracy**, **control** and **obedience**. Some can
indeed be quite skinny, and the risk of a run-out is very high.
The approach should be made in a well-engaged canter
without too much **speed**.

By keeping the canter **engaged** the risk of a run-out

should be reduced, as the rider will retain control right to
the face of the fence. Galloping in on a fast, strung-out
stride could allow the horse to run out as he takes the control from his rider.

A long stride will also increase inaccuracy. Standing way
off the fence could also allow the horse the opportunity to
'duck' out at the last minute.

The rider should sit well up all the way to the fence and
should not topple forward or drop the horse's balance.

To ride straight to an arrowhead it is important to ride
forward, just like when riding the centre line at the start of
a dressage test. Pulling against the horse will encourage
resistance, crookedness and loss of control of the hindquarters.

I do not tend to over-practice arrowheads in training. One
or two occasionally for assurance is fine, but I prefer instead
to ensure straightness by using exercises (angled lines, offset doubles, etc.) over wider fences where the margin for

error is slightly more lenient. Do not attempt arrowheads
until straightness and an engaged canter can be achieved
as creating run-out problems will set back confidence.

■ PHOTO ANALYSIS

Photo 1 The approach is made with control and engagement.
The rider displays a nice independence of balance with his
weight well down into his heel. The horse is nicely supported in the rider's hands to prevent a run-out but the
presentation is still forward with no resistance shown.

Photo 2 The take-off is accurate as a result of the engaged
stride pattern. Galloping in on a long stride and standing
well off an arrowhead is risky as a loss of control may occur.

Photo 3 The jump is very straight and ...

Photo 4 ... the horse lands balanced and confident. The
rider is already thinking about the next fence and lands
softly with good security through his stirrup.

Combinations

Key points
Rhythm maintained through all elements.
Careful analysis of line and distances.

■ IDEAL TECHNIQUE

Combination fences should be taken with an overall **rhythm** from beginning to end.

The separate elements should flow together and not be treated as a series of unconnected efforts. Throughout the combination there should be no obvious or immediate break in the forward momentum, and each of the individual 'problems' presented should be given general consideration in relation to one another.

For example, where the combination may consist of a wide spread (first) followed by an upright (second), the approach to the spread should reflect the fact that consideration has been given to the upright as well. Perhaps the normal impulsion and lengthening will be a touch more controlled in readiness for the upright that follows.

Any alterations to pace should be subtle.

The distance between fences in combinations should be carefully studied when walking the course so the rider has complete understanding of the striding requirements.

He needs to consider not only how many strides to take but also whether they are short, requiring control and engagement, or whether they are long, needing boldness and scope.

The most sensible line through the entire combination should also be established.

Upright to Spread

■ PHOTO ANALYSIS

A combination fence consisting of upright rails with one stride to a corner. This is a question that requires some control on the approach and then plenty of impulsion for the spread fence out.

Photo 1 Here the rider has made a careful and controlled approach to the vertical. She has been rewarded with a clean jump.

Photo 2 However, the horse appears to have remained short in his frame and tight in his jump, indicating that con-

trol on the approach may have been exaggerated. The horse also appears to be drifting to the left and the rider has lost her lower leg backwards.

Photo 3 Consequently an extreme effort has been needed to ensure that one stride is executed instead of two. The rider runs the risk of a run-out by being too far off the fence and by throwing the hands forward. The horse is not in front of the rider's leg. The sequence of jumps may have been improved with a more rhythmic flow between the two.

Upright to Bounce

▣ IDEAL TECHNIQUE

See Combinations.

▣ PHOTO ANALYSIS

Photo 2 At the early stage in the approach to this combination, things are not going well. The rider is very aware of the need for a greater degree of control if she is to hold her line through all three parts of the fence and have sufficient engagement to negotiate the bounce successfully. The horse is resisting her attempts to slow him down.

Photo 3 At the point of take-off there are still some last-minute alterations occurring. There is a small correction of line with the right rein, so the horse is slightly crooked instead of straight between each rein. The rider has accepted the pace as the best she can manage and has stopped pulling against the horse to ensure that she is not disrupting his focus on the fence. She is sitting well.

Photo 4 Having negotiated the first element, horse and rider are now acting far more as one.

Photo 5 The jump into the bounce appears to be very bold. The rider is still sitting well and endeavouring to regulate the speed quietly, without interfering too much.

Photo 6 The horse is aware of the last element of the bounce and is shortening his bascule nicely while still remaining careful in his jump. The rider is sitting well back, which may indicate that she is still travelling quite quickly.

Photo 7 The final element is successfully negotiated, with perhaps the fence itself backing the horse off as much as the rider. She has done well not to get into a 'tug of war' with her horse.

Ditch and Palisade Drop to Palisade

▓ IDEAL TECHNIQUE

See Combinations

▓ PHOTO ANALYSIS

Photo 1 My approach to the ditch and palisade has been quite strong, perhaps even a little too powerful. I have brought the horse close to the fence to ensure that he doesn't need to launch himself into the air too much. Resting my hands on his neck is not good as I run the risk of 'dropping' his balance or losing the engagement.

Photo 2 I am aware now that I have generated too much power for the drop fence so I am already thinking of helping my horse for the next element of the combination. I am sitting up and giving the horse only the rein that he needs to jump fluently; at the same time I am hoping to slow him down. I have let my leg come forward as an emergency measure in case I am unsuccessful in gaining control in time.

Photo 3 I have come a bit too close to the fence for comfort, although the horse has done a good job of protecting himself. I have fallen too low with my shoulders and have had to let my elbows stick out to take up the slack in my reins.

2

Related Fences

■ IDEAL TECHNIQUE

See Combinations

■ PHOTO ANALYSIS

Photo 1 Here we have two fences on a related line with four strides between the two elements. The first fence, an upright wall, must be taken on an angle to provide an ideal line to the corner that follows. The horse is making a positive jump into the combination and the rider is already looking to the next fence.

Photo 2 As soon as the horse lands into the related distance the rider drives on effectively. The most important stride in any related distance is the first one. This rider has not wasted a stride in generating some forward power here.

Photo 3 She has made the distance work nicely for her and has brought the horse up close to the second fence on her fourth stride with the accuracy, power and engagement needed to negotiate the corner.

Photo 4 The resulting jump is straight and fluent. The rider has maintained an excellent position.

Sunken Road

Key points

Treated as a combination so an overall rhythm is essential.

Short, controlled stride on approach.

Impulsion and engagement on way out.

■ IDEAL TECHNIQUE

A sunken road should be approached with a similar technique to jumping a **coffin**. The speed should not be too fast to give the horse time to assess the problems ahead. The stride should be **controlled** and well **engaged** but with plenty of **impulsion**. A short, bouncy stride but with lots of revs is required.

The rider should sit up to avoid getting caught ahead of the movement and should keep the horse's balance well supported all the way to the fence. He should not drop the horse onto his forehand in front of the fence and he should keep his leg on to avoid a refusal.

Once over the first set of rails the rider must continue to ride each element as it is required and should maintain a light seat and an independence of balance throughout. He should encourage a positive jump down into the road, allowing sufficient freedom through the reins for the horse to jump fluently, but should not slip them to the extent that he loses all connection and control. The stride in the bottom should be treated with quick reactions to ensure the horse has the engagement and power for the jump up the bank and the fence that follows. The rider should look ahead to the next element at all times.

The sequence should be ridden as a combination, so there should be a flowing rhythm from start to finish.

■ PHOTO ANALYSIS

Example

Photo 1 This rider sits in a secure balance over the first element of this sunken road complex. He is close to the saddle and has his weight well distributed over the centre of the horse's balance. He has brought his shoulders back to prevent him getting caught ahead of the movement.

The approach speed and the engagement of the stride must have been about correct, as although the horse's attention is very obviously already on the drop down, he is still executing a clean jump over the upright rails.

Photo 2 The horse lands onto the bank and then must immediately bounce down the step that follows. The rider has taken the impact of the landing on his stirrups and has begun to slip his reins to allow the horse freedom to balance himself and remain forward in his motion.

Photo 3 Having remained in a good balance throughout the first two photos, in the third the rider begins to get slightly ahead of the movement. His slipped reins have now become long reins, which could result in a loss of control, steering and engagement.

Photo 4 It appears that the impulsion has dwindled so the rider has become active with both his legs and his seat. The horse lacks the connection of his frame, indicated by the looseness of the reins, to produce the powerful jump up the bank that is needed.

Photo 5 With positive riding the energy is being regained, although the horse still pokes his nose out in front and his hocks are trailing behind.

Photo 6 Sufficient energy has been generated to ensure a fluent last jump. During the entire sequence the rider has had his eyes trained on the exit jump over each separate element, and this has ensured his positive ride to the end.

Fence with Roof

Key points

The horse must not be rushed in his approach.

Engaged and well-connected stride.

Rider must think positively but ride defensively.

■ IDEAL TECHNIQUE

A fence with a roof above it should not be taken too fast. The stride should be well connected and the horse should be given plenty of time to assess his surroundings before making his jump. He should not be **rushed**, especially if the roof casts a shadow over the fence itself.

Many horses will lose a little confidence with the confinement of space and may not get the height that would normally be expected at a straightforward fence. With experience they learn to overcome these concerns and gain confidence.

The rider should sit up and, although he should remain positive and attacking, he should also think defensively, sitting up in the approach so as to avoid getting ahead of the movement.

The stride should not be excessively long but should remain sufficiently engaged to ensure that the horse arrives accurately at the fence. Standing well off should be avoided.

■ PHOTO ANALYSIS

A solid table fence with a low roof above, made more difficult because the approach requires moving from light into dark.

Photo 1 The horse appears a fraction suspicious of the question as the rider is slightly behind the centre of balance and has dropped close to the saddle. The horse is backing off.

Photo 2 The point of take-off seems normal, although the rider needs to bring his seat and shoulders forward to stay with the movement. This can be a problem if something goes wrong during the jump or the forward momentum of the horse is stalled.

Photo 3 The horse suddenly shows concern about the roof above his head and fails to jump up as much as he usually would. Instead he crouches over the fence. This can be a normal reaction for many horses until they gain confidence with this type of fence. As the rider got behind the balance initially to persuade the horse forward in the approach he has now got too much in front of the movement.

Photo 4 A successful completion.

Turning Fences

Key points

Controlled approach with not too much speed.
Rider must look ahead in direction he wants to go.
Horse and rider to maintain balance and rhythm
throughout.

▣ IDEAL TECHNIQUE

Fences that require changes of direction in the approach
should be ridden with **control** and not with too much speed.

Balance and rhythm should not only be maintained at the
jumps but are also essential throughout the turn.

Many riders will struggle to gain control once they have
already begun making their turn. This is often too late. If the
speed can be reduced first, the horse will come round the
turn more easily – much as a car and trailer will if the driver
brakes first, then turns and accelerates out of the turn.

The rider will need to look and think ahead of where he
actually is in order to be prepared in time for the next chal-
lenge. More often than not, where we look is where we go,
so looking ahead will help.

Flatwork training will be rewarded at these types of
fences. The horse will need to be supple and responsive.

The rider should guide the horse in the turn with both reins
and should not just pull excessively on the inside one. This
will often have an adverse effect as the horse loses his balance through the outside shoulder or swings his quarters.

Serpentine

▣ PHOTO ANALYSIS

Photo 2 A good start to this sequence of turning fences.
Horse and rider are jumping the first element straight but
are already thinking ahead to the second effort. The rider's
eyes are trained on the next jump and she is indicating to
her horse that they will be turning left. This will enable him

to land with his left foreleg leading thus making the turn
smooth and balanced.

Photo 3 The first turn is made with control ...

Photo 4 ... but the spread of the second element takes the
rider a bit by surprise and ...

Photo 5 ... she slips the reins to absorb the big effort made
by the horse. She has indicated to the horse that there is a
change of direction ahead, with her body weight, and she is
still looking ahead to the next fence. However, she has lost
her lower leg backwards over the fence so ...

Photo 6 ... does not land securely herself and is momentarily unbalanced. She has now lost a degree of control but
she has not lost her focus on the last element and has not
given up trying to get there.

Photo 7 Despite the long reins the rider has worked hard
to recover her own balance and to re-engage the horse. She
has continued through the complex on a consistent rhythm
and ...

Photo 8 ... is rewarded with a successful negotiation of the
obstacle.

Hair-Pin Turn

■ PHOTO ANALYSIS

Photo 1 As the rider lands over the first element of this two-part combination with a hair-pin turn in between, she is already beginning to check the control. Her hands are braced, her leg is forward and her shoulders are raised. She will want to ensure she has maximum control before she begins her turn, rather than be struggling to steady the pace as she alters her direction.

Photo 2 The horse appears to be a little strong here but the rider stays up with her body and already she is looking ahead to where she wants to go. (She does not need to look at the trees as she goes around them. She has walked her course and knows her line between the two elements.) Her shoulders are level in the turn. She is not leaning in on the corner, affecting her horse's balance.

Photo 3 The rider's eyes are still very much looking ahead. The horse has completed the turn in balance. The rider has not simply pulled the horse around with her inside rein only, but has guided the horse with both reins, supported him with both legs and has used her body effectively too.

Photo 4 A picture of total control and security. The turn between the two elements has not disrupted the rhythm or imposed itself on the outcome of the final jump.

Diagonal Line

Key points
Accuracy and control.
Engaged stride.
Eyes on correct line.

■ IDEAL TECHNIQUE

On some occasions it is not possible to ride straight at the face of a fence - for example, when riding at fences in the woods or tackling offset doubles. It will then be necessary to hold a straight line diagonally across the face of the jump.

The approach should be similar to when riding arrow-heads or corners. It should be with **engagement** and **control**.

The stride pattern should be short to ensure **accuracy**. If the stride is long and fast then the rider may lose control and suffer a run-out.

The horse should dissect the fence on an angle and should not deviate to follow the direction of the fence itself. He should not drift off a straight line in the air.

The rider should keep his shoulders and eyes up.

■ PHOTO ANALYSIS

Example 1

Here is a single fence approached on an acute angle.

Photo 1a The horse is backing off slightly as he is pre-sented deep to the base of the fence. This has been done to reduce the risk of a run-out or to prevent the horse from drifting crooked in the air.

I am sitting with my shoulders well up, and although I am close to the saddle with my seat, most of my weight remains in my stirrup.

The horse has plenty of freedom, as can be seen by the fact that his nose is stretched forward, but I have not dropped the contact. The horse is channelled between both legs and both hands.

Photo 1b The horse holds his line nicely in the air and ignores the direction of the fence. He responds instead to my guidance. Throughout I have kept my eyes ahead, on the line I wish to take.

Photo 1c The horse lands on the same line without devia-tion. I have taken the impact of landing through my stirrup.

Example 2

Photo 2a A front view of the same fence taken on a different approach. The speed has been increased and the stride is now much longer. I have fixed my hands down with rigid elbows and as a result the horse is resisting my attempts to engage him. It is evident in this photo that he is already becoming crooked by pushing his weight out through his shoulder.

Photo 2b By standing off the fence and with too much speed I have lost my control and accuracy and have com-pletely drifted off my line. The horse has jumped towards the face of the fence instead of maintaining the straight-ness that should have dissected the fence on an angle.

Open Ditch or Water

Key points
Bold, lengthening stride.
Horse in front of the rider's leg.
Engagement to create power.

◼ IDEAL TECHNIQUE

An open ditch or water should be approached on a **powerful**, **attacking** stride, especially if the hazard is wide. The gallop should be full of **impulsion** and, as is the case with all spread fences, the open ditch should be met on a **lengthening stride**. The power should not diminish in the last few strides nor should the strides begin to shorten.

Although boldness is required, the speed should **not** be too **fast** or the horse may be unable to digest the problem and will be surprised at the last minute by the hole in the ground.

Accuracy of take-off is important as there will be nothing for the horse to sight his distance against, so the rider must retain some engagement of the stride. If the horse is completely strung out he will have no containment of his 'spring' and the take-off spot might become inaccurate. The horse will gain more distance if he jumps upwards rather than diving in a flat manner.

If the rider feels that the horse is not increasing in impulsion and length of stride, he could introduce a touch of his whip immediately behind his leg to reinforce the need to go forward. The whip should be applied only behind the heel as an extension of the rider's leg aids. Slapping the horse on the shoulder really only reassures the rider and does not educate the horse to respect the leg.

The rider should look up, not down, and the horse should be encouraged to do the same.

◼ PHOTO ANALYSIS

Example 1

Photo 1 A happy combination clearing an open ditch with ease. The horse has gained good height in his jump which will in turn carry him well out over the back of the ditch. The rider appears to have met the take-off spot on a lengthening stride to ensure boldness but has not lost the connection between her hand and the horse's mouth, thereby retaining the engagement and impulsion needed to gener-

ate some scope and power. Both horse and rider are looking up and not down into the bottom of the ditch, although the rider may have been surprised a bit by the horse's extravagant jump, and as a result she has lost some of the security in her lower leg.

Example 2

Photo 2 Both horse and rider appear unconcerned by this open ditch, but the jump appears a bit flat and hollow. The rider does not have the same good line from his elbow to the horse's mouth that can be seen in the previous photo, indicating a lack of power and impulsion. The stride may have been totally lengthened in the approach instead of lengthening. The rider's shoulders are lower than I would consider ideal.

Example 3

Photo 3 Although this combination have successfully negotiated the open ditch, my main concern with this picture is the length of the rider's stirrup leathers. They are too long. Many riders presume that a long stirrup will give them added security, whereas in reality the opposite is often the case.

Here there is insufficient angle in the knee to absorb the impact of landing well. The foot has slipped through the stirrup and the rider appears to be taking some balance on her hands, which are braced on the horse's neck. The position of the rider can become loose when the security is not in the lower leg.

Start Box

Key points

Rider must remain calm with no sudden movements or reactions.

Keep the horse walking and relaxed until called into the box.

Be well prepared in advance.

■ IDEAL TECHNIQUE

Consideration should be given to ensuring that the starting procedure is addressed in a sensible and efficient manner. Many competitions have been lost at the beginning by horse or rider failing to maximise the start, or even failing to start at all.

It is always a time of intense pressure and pent-up anxieties, but it will not help to get 'wound up' about the start. Instead it should be approached in a relaxed and systematic way.

If the rider educates the horse to remain calm at all his early competitions, he should not incur any long-term hang-ups. If, on the other hand, he is late arriving, hurried, anxious or dramatic in his actions, this can create a myriad of escalating problems which can prove difficult to resolve.

The rider will nearly always be warned when there is about one minute or thirty seconds till his starting time. Sometimes it will be both. Prior to this the horse should be walking quietly nearby to the start box. Girth straps should be tightened and/or stirrups adjusted well before now.

The horse will not know that he is about to gallop off unless his rider sends him exciting 'messages' through his own actions. With fifteen to twenty seconds to go, the horse should be moved closer and walked quietly into the box itself to stand. Occasionally when educating my young horses I will even walk them into the box, stand and walk back out again, providing that I have plenty of time to utilise.

Once given the command to 'go!' the rider should begin gradually. The time for a sprint start is later in the horse's career, when a split second will matter, not at the beginning.

■ PHOTO ANALYSIS

Photo 1 Once given the call by the starter, the rider, who has been walking her horse quietly nearby, moves towards the start box. She is choosing to enter through the side of the box. If preferred, it is still permissible to enter through the wider front entrance.

Photo 2 Although the rider is already looking towards the first fence it is obvious that the horse is looking elsewhere in a relaxed and happy manner. He is on a soft contact so is not nervous or wound up. (However, they appear to be standing in the gateway, which possibly isn't such a good idea - any unexpected sudden swing from the horse could result in horse or rider hitting the rails end-on.)

Photo 3 When the countdown is completed and the command to go given, the rider turns quietly and moves off gradually. There is no sudden or dramatic rush. Her hand is offered forward to 'release the hand brake' at the same time as the accelerator (her leg) is applied.

Photo 4 As a result a sensible and efficient start is made.

Part 4 **Problems**

Refusal

Key points
Rider must keep weight into the heel and eyes and shoulders up.

Quickly analyse the reason and rectify, e.g. better line, slower approach, more impulsion.

If the horse needs reprimanding then use the whip immediately and directly behind the leg.

■ DESCRIPTION

The odd refusal, although disappointing, will be inevitable in cross-country, especially in the early stages of a horse or rider's education. Refusals are not the end of the world and should be treated as part of the learning process.

They can occur for any number of reasons. Loss of confidence (horse or rider), loss of balance, loss of impulsion, loss of engagement, approaching too slowly, approaching too fast, presenting on a bad line, etc.

It always amuses me to hear a good rider analysing a refusal. He will always say 'I wish I had done 'this' or 'that' instead,' working out what he could have done better in his attempt. A poor rider almost always blames the horse!

Once a rider can identify a justifiable reason for the refusal, he can usually fix it by making the necessary correction – e.g. stronger if the approach was weak, straighter if crooked, better balanced, etc.

Having said that the odd refusal is inevitable, they should not be accepted as commonplace. If the horse is being ungenuine and refusing doggedly then he should be taught otherwise before it becomes a bad habit. Excessive speed should never be used but clear and simple persuasion enforced. I never use my whip anywhere other than imme-

diately behind my leg to educate the horse that it is used as an extension to my leg aids. Hopefully he will learn to respect the leg as a result.

If a refusal occurs the rider should not fall off. If the rider's weight is well into the heels, he is gripping strongly with his calves and his eyes and shoulders are up, then he should stay on. If the shoulders are going forward and the lower leg is sliding back, there is a strong possibility that horse and rider will be parted.

■ PHOTO ANALYSIS

Photo 1 This inexperienced horse pops over the small log that precedes a water fence but he already shows concern about the water itself. He is pushing left through his shoulder, and because the rider is not looking ahead she does not register the change in direction soon enough. The approach may have been a fraction too fast.

Photo 2 The line into the water is now less than ideal, so the rider needs to correct the horse's straightness at the same time as riding him forward.

Photo 3 A refusal has occurred. Despite the rider's determination, the horse proves the stronger of the two.

Photo 4 On the second attempt the approach is made further towards the middle and on a straighter line. The approach is made more slowly so the rider can maintain control and guide the horse straight, and when he hesitates she can drive him forwards. She keeps her bodyweight well up.

Photo 5 With all other options closed, the horse responds to his rider's wishes and lowers himself into the water. Success was achieved by gaining control, correcting straightness and restoring balance.

Photo 6 With the education repeated several more times the horse is soon jumping confidently into water without hesitation. Here the rider sits in a secure seat.

Run-Out

■ DESCRIPTION

A run-out is usually the result of a **loss of control** but can also be the result of a bad line, nervousness or lack of balance.

If there is a contest of strength between horse and rider then the horse will nearly always win. He is so much bigger.

Therefore, for the rider to prevent the horse from taking control, and to be able to influence his direction, he must ensure he has the upper hand. Greater engagement and a reduction of the speed should increase the rider's effectiveness.

Running out can also be the result of a disobedience from the horse. If it goes uncorrected it can develop into a major problem. If, for example, the horse runs out to the left, the rider should first stop him from running away from the problem, and turn him back to the front of the fence with the right rein. The rider should not just continue around on the line the horse chooses. Once in front of the fence the horse can be reprimanded before a second attempt. Hopefully the horse will understand that he has done wrong, and instead of repeating the run-out he will look for a way over

the fence rather than around it. He should be rewarded immediately he jumps.

■ PHOTO ANALYSIS

Photo 1 The approach to this wide corner is being made on a long, galloping stride. The rider is urging strongly with her legs, but her heel has come up so the effectiveness of her lower leg is lost. She has let her shoulders drop too far forward in front of the fence. The horse is resisting her hands and is raising his head, removing his focus from the fence. The last stride will not bring them close to the base of the jump.

Photo 2 Despite the gallant attempt by the rider to hold the horse straight with her left rein, he has pushed his body-weight out through his right shoulder. He has simply turned his head and neck towards the left.

Photo 3 A run-out has occurred. (I am sure that the spooky-looking scarecrow sitting on the fence has not helped matters!) The horse has taken the control away from his rider. A more engaged stride with less speed and more control produced a successful result at the second attempt.

Fall

DESCRIPTION

From time to time a fall will occur as a result of a misjudgement, either by the horse or the rider. It is not possible to be perfect all of the time.

Most riders accept that falls are part and parcel of the challenges of cross-country riding. If the rider is unduly worried about the potential for a fall then he should not be riding cross-country at all. It is not for the faint-hearted.

Falls can cause a loss of confidence but they should not be dwelt on for too long. Each fall should be analysed to work out the cause and then it should be learnt from and promptly placed in the past.

▓ PHOTO ANALYSIS

Photo 1 Here the rider is making a rapid approach to the fence. The horse has lost his balance and engagement. Even though all four of his feet are off the ground, he appears to be lowering his body.

Photo 2 Because of the loss of balance, the horse needs to slam on the brakes at the very last minute. He has become too disengaged, with his frame too extended to make a good jump.

Photo 3 The rider has shot up the horse's neck as a result of the sudden stop to the horse's momentum.

Photo 4 The pace has been such that the horse has been unable to stop in time. A fall has occurred. Thankfully neither horse nor rider was hurt and both were able to put this unfortunate incident behind them, regaining confidence to go on to future success.

Glossary

Against the hand
When the horse ignores the rider's hands as a means of control or steering, leaning on the reins instead. A lack of submission.

Ahead of the movement
When the rider is in front of the horse's centre of balance. Undesirable across country as it will mean that the rider is in a vulnerable position if the forward momentum is checked.

Backing off
When the horse severely reduces the length of his frame or steps in the approach strides to an obstacle. Often associated with spooky or unwilling horses and may cause refusals or falls.

Bascule
The arc or parabola in which the horse jumps. Likely to be longer or flatter across country than in show jumping as a result of the increased speed and more open stride of the gallop.

Behind the leg
When the horse is reluctant to move forward freely from the rider's leg aids, resulting in the rider needing to urge him constantly. The opposite effect is desirable where a horse 'in front of the leg' will willingly 'take' his rider across country without constant reminding.

Centre of balance
The point of the horse over which the rider should distribute as much of his own weight as possible. This point will move forwards on the horse when the galloping stride gets longer, and will shift back towards the quarters when the stride is condensed or the speed reduced.

Chipping in
Adding an additional small stride before take-off at the face of a jump. Usually the result of a lack of balance, engagement or control. Could cause a loss of rhythm or power and usually produces an awkward jump.

Coiled spring
Another description for engagement. Often also referred to as a 'coffin canter'. The impulsion and energy have been created by the rider and are contained between hand and leg.

Elasticity
Suppleness and smoothness of paces, engagement and control in the horse. Without rigidity or stiffness. A lack of elasticity can create resistance and stiffness in either horse or rider.

Engagement
The connection of the horse's frame and stride. With engagement the rider should feel that the balance is round and uphill and that the horse's hindquarters are controlled in his hands.

Impulsion
Most easily described as 'contained energy'. Not to be confused with speed. The power is harnessed in the rider's hand, giving the ability to increase pace or extend the stride without loss of control or balance. Impulsion is created from engagement.

On the forehand
When the centre of balance is too far forward and too low; the weight of the horse is all on the shoulders or reliant on the rider's hands, and the balance is not on the hindquarters. Not recommended at any time but especially not in the approach to cross-country fences, as being on the forehand can greatly increase the chances of a fall.

Resistance
The horse is not accepting the rider's aids and stiffens against the hand. Often the greatest cause of horse resistance is restriction. Frequently will cause a raised head carriage and a hollow outline.

Slipping the reins
Allowing the reins to slide through the rider's fingers to give sufficient freedom to the horse to extend his neck when needed. Often necessary when jumping drop fences or during awkward situations where the horse is required to adjust his balance.

Standing off
Taking off at an obstacle too far from the ideal point – usually the result of a lack of control and engagement, or too much speed.

Stickability
The ability of the rider to make quick and dramatic movements to regain his independent balance, and remain on the horse in an awkward situation.

Index

accuracy
  arrowhead 89
  corner fences 48-9
  diagonal line 106
  hayrack fence 83
after-care of horse 29
ahead of the movement 11, 37
angle, jumping on 106-7
Animalintex 30
approach
  diagonal line 106-7
  drop fence 84
  and refusals 112
  speed 56, 68, 72, 84, 102
  straightness 48-9
arms, rider's 12
arnica 30
arrowhead 88-9

back protector 23
balance
  bounces 77, 79
  downhill fence 52-3
  horse 13
  rider 10-12, 46, 77, 79, 99
  steps down 46-7
bandages 21
bank
  down 64-7
  out of water 68, 69, 71
  up 60-3
behind the movement 11, 44-5, 56, 74
bits 14, 21
boldness 15-17
boots
  horse 21, 22
  rider 24
  whirlpool 30
bounces 76-81
  in combination fence 92-3
  ideal technique 77
  into water 80-1
breastplate 21, 22
bridles 20
bruising 30
bullfinch 58-9

changes of direction 102-5
coffin fence 17, 54-7
coiled spring 36, 37, 77, 83
cold hosing 29
combinations
  ditch and palisade drop to palisade 94-5
  ideal technique 90-1
  related fences 96-7
  upright to bounce 92-3
  upright to spread 90-1
  see also coffin fence; sunken road
commitment, of rider 17
confidence
  building 15-17
  and falls 116
connection
  corner fences 48-9
  fence on upward slope 50-1
  hanging log 38
  upright fences 32
contact 12
control 14, 21
  arrowhead fence 89
  and bits 14, 21
  coffin fence 54, 56
  corner fences 48-9
  and run-outs 14, 89, 114-15
  and speed 17
  steps down 46-7
  turning fences 102
  upright fences 32-3
cooling horse down 29
corner fences 48-9
  building confidence 15
  ideal technique 48
  run-out 115
countdown 110
course walk 25-7, 90-1

defensive riding 35, 38-9, 74, 80-1, 86
diagonal line 106-7
distances, combination fences 90-1
ditch 15, 17, 40-3
  ideal technique 40
  open 108-9
  with palisade 40-1

training the young horse 15, 17, 40
  trakehner 42-3
downhill slope 13, 52-3
drop fences 64-7, 84-7
  in combination 94-5
  ideal technique 84-5
  into water 68, 70, 72-3, 74
  log 85, 86-7
  palisade 86

eggbutt snaffle 21
engagement 13, 14
  arrowhead fence 89
  bounces 77
  corner fences 48-9
  downhill fence 52-3
  upright fences 32
equipment
  horse 20-3
  rider 23-5
  ten-minute box 28
experience, cross-country 17
eyes, rider's 40, 60-1, 98, 99, 102, 104-5, 108-9

falls 116-17
false ground-line 82-3
fears, overcoming 15
fence with roof 100-1
first aid, horse 29-30
fitness, horse/rider 25
flash noseband 20
flow 35, 37
forehand, horse on 14, 52-3
French link snaffle 21

gag bits 21
gates 33
girths 20
gloves 24
grease, leg 23, 28
ground-line 36
  false 82-3
  fences without 33, 38-9

hair-pin turn 104-5
hanging log 38-9

hayrack 82-3
hedge, bullfinch 58-9
helmets 23
horse
  after-care 29
  balance 13
  boldness and confidence 15-17
  control of 14, 21
  equipment 20-3
  fitness 25
  injuries 25, 29-30
  novice, see novice horse
  trust in rider 17-18
hosing, cold 29

ice boots 29
impulsion 14, 15
  bank down 64
  bank up and fence 60-1
  bounces 77, 79
  ditches 40
  spread fences 35
  steps up 44-5
injuries, horse 25, 29-30
interval training 25

kaolin clay 30
knees, rider's 11, 42, 109

leg grease 23, 28
lengthening stride 35, 40, 84, 108
light seat 44, 45, 61
log
  on downhill slope 52-3
  with drop 85, 86-7
  hanging 38-9
  into water 74
  simple 36-7
looking ahead 102, 104-5
looking down 40
looking up 60-1, 108
lower leg, rider's 11, 58-9, 86, 87, 109, 112, 115

martingales 20-1, 77
medical card 24

nosebands 20
novice horse 15, 17
    coffin fence 54-7
    ditches 15, 17, 40
    spread fence 35
    steps 18, 44-5
    water fences 17, 18
number bib 24

open ditch/water 108-9
over-reach boots 21, 22
oxer, square 35

pace, assessment 17
palisade
    after bank up 60-1
    and ditch 40
    with drop 86
pelham, vulcanite 21
physiotherapy 30
poultices 30
power 14
    coffin fence 54
    fence on upward slope 50-1
    spread fences 35
    steps up 44-5
    see also impulsion
problems
    falls 116-17
    refusals 112-13
    run-out 14, 114-15

racing breastplate 21, 22
refusals 112-13
reins
    knotting 20
    slipping 39, 45, 46, 74, 84, 85, 98-9
    types 20
related fences 96-7
rhythm 15, 36, 38, 51, 58, 90, 99
rider
    commitment 17
    confidence 15
    equipment 23-5
    eyes 40, 60-1, 98, 99, 102, 104-5, 108-9
    fitness 25
rider's position 10-12, 20
    ahead of the movement 11, 37
    balance 10-12, 46-7, 77, 79
    behind the movement 11, 44-5, 56, 74
    defensive 35, 38-9, 74, 80-1, 86
    light seat 44, 45, 61
    lower leg 11, 58-9, 86, 87, 109, 112, 115
    and security 10-12, 42-3, 84-5, 109, 112

shoulders 11, 64-5, 109, 114-15
roof, over fence 100-1
rubber stoppers 20
run-outs
    causes 14, 89, 114
    prevention 114-15
running martingale 20-1, 77

saddles 20, 22, 23
schooling 14
security of rider 10-12, 112
    drop fences 84-5
    and stirrup length 11, 42-3, 109
serpentine fence 102-3
shoulder pads 23
shoulders, rider's 11, 64-5, 109, 114-15
simple log 36-7
slipping reins 39, 45, 46-7, 74, 84, 85, 98-9
slopes
    downward 13, 52-3
    upward 50-1
snaffle bits 21
speed 14, 17
    drop fence 84
    fence with a roof 100
    judging 17
    open ditch/water 108
    turning fences 102
    water fences 68, 72
spread fences 34-5
'spring' 36, 37, 77, 79, 83
spurs 24
standing martingale 21
standing off, ditch 40-1
start box 28, 110-11
steps
    down 46-7
    training novice horse 18
    up 44
'stickability' 46-7
stirrups 20
    length for cross-country 11, 42-3, 109
stitching, checking 20
stopwatch 24
straightness
    arrowhead fence 89
    corner fences 48-9
    diagonal line 106-7
stride
    jumping out of 36-7, 58
    length and balance 13
    lengthening 35, 40, 84, 108
studs 23
sunken road 98-9

sweet-iron gag 21

take-off spot
    ditch 40-1
    fence with poor/false ground-line 38-9, 82-3
    fence on upward slope 50-1
    open ditch or water 108
    spread fences 35
    upright fences 32-3
ten-minute box procedure 28, 29
tendon injuries 29
three-ring gag 21
times, fast 17
training
    advanced horse 18
    coffin 17
    ditches 15, 17, 40
    novice horse 17-18
    water fences 17, 18, 68
trakehner 42-3
trust, horse in rider 17-18
Tubigrip 30
turning fences
    hair-pin 104-5
    ideal technique 102
    serpentine 102-3

upright fences
    followed by bank down 64-7
    ideal technique 32-3
Uptite 30
upward slope 50-1

veterinary inspections 28
veterinary kit 30
vulcanite pelham 21

walking the course 25-7, 90-1
watch 24
water 68-75
    bounce into 80-1
    ideal technique 68
    open 108-9
    refusals 112-13
    training young horse 17, 18, 68
whip
    cross-country type 23
    use of 17, 23, 108, 112
whirlpool boots 30